Practical Saddle Fitting

Practical Saddle Fitting

Ken Lyndon-Dykes

J.A. ALLEN · LONDON

© Ken Lyndon-Dykes, 2005
First published in Great Britain 2005

ISBN 0 85131 852 5

J.A. Allen
Clerkenwell House
Clerkenwell Green
London ECIR OHT

J.A. Allen is an imprint of Robert Hale Limited

A catalogue record for this book is available from the British Library

Photographs by the author, except for the photograph of the
Tri-form tree (page 13), reproduced with permission of the manufacturers

Edited by Martin Diggle
Design and typesetting by Paul Saunders
Line illustrations by Dick Vine

Colour separation by Tenon & Polert Colour Scanning Limited, Hong Kong
Printed by New Era Printing Company Ltd, Hong Kong China

Dedication

This book is dedicated to the memory of A.W. (Tony) Russell,
Fellow of the Society of Master Saddlers who, for ten years, gave exemplary
service as Chief Executive of the Society of Master Saddlers.

Contents

Acknowledgements

I wish to acknowledge that this book could not have been written without the help, guidance and expertise of my dear friend Pat Crawford distinguished equestrian journalist. She is, in every real sense, the co-author of this book, but modesty has prevented her from taking joint credit for it, despite several attempts to persuade her to do so.

I would also like to acknowledge the work and support of the following people:

Dennis Colton, Fellow of the Society of Master Saddlers, the rock upon whose shoulders the organization of and responsibility for the saddle fitting course was carried.

Julia Steel-Morgan, Fellow of the Society of Master Saddlers and former President, under whose presidency the saddle fitting course was instituted.

Kay Hastilow, Master Saddler SMS, my fellow course leader, tutor and examiner.

Paul Belton, former President SMS, distinguished saddle designer and innovator.

Laura Dempsey SMS, side-saddle specialist.

Sandie Panek SMS (USA).

Introduction

Saddling is a craft, a science and an art.

The *craft* lies in the tradition and in the appreciation of superb workmanship.

The *science* is in the design, foresight and innovation and usage of modern materials.

The *art* is making the right decision.

Saddles are Merely a Convenience – Not a Necessity

This may seem a strange statement with which to introduce a book on saddle fitting, but it is, nonetheless, true. Early cave paintings depict riders sitting in the centre of their horse's balance unaided by a saddle: the Native Americans exhibited amazing balance and suppleness on horseback that was not dependent on assistance from a saddle. For centuries, circus riders have demonstrated remarkable agility and suppleness that had no dependence on a saddle. Young children, riding bareback, frequently exhibit total fearlessness and remarkable poise. The Pony Club vaulting teams reach an enviably high standard of performance in a sport that would actually be hindered by the addition of saddles.

Over many centuries, saddles have been designed to assist riders to perform better in differing situations in a multiplicity of disciplines. The only benefit derived by the horse relates to the saddle's ability to assist the rider to maintain a position that is the least possible hindrance to his mount's natural balance. Essentially, it is the rider – not the horse – who needs the saddle. The best designed, most beautifully crafted saddle made specifically to fit an individual horse will not improve the horse's ability to perform, benefit his welfare or increase his comfort. Conversely, however, the saddle that is badly designed, poorly crafted and fits inadequately can seriously and adversely affect the horse's comfort and welfare and impair his ability to perform. Protracted use of a badly fitting saddle may, in extreme cases, cause irreversible physical problems. Simply expressed – the best saddle is a compromise, a useful tool for the rider. So far as the horse is concerned, it is an instrument of damage limitation

Why is it so Important for a Saddle to Fit Properly?

This question is so fundamental it makes one wonder why the importance of a well-fitting saddle has, generally speaking, only been understood in recent times. But it is a fact that, only twenty years or so ago – all over the world – it was common practice for horse owners to walk into their local saddlers, pick a few saddles they liked the look of and 'try' them on a saddle-horse. The most comfortable was then purchased, taken home and put on the horse. It was, in fact, quite common practice to use the same saddle on several horses of differing conformation – factors such as high withers (and sore backs!) being addressed by the addition of rugs, pads, numnahs, pieces of sponge and other paraphernalia placed beneath the saddle. There was little understanding that such indiscriminate insertions could seriously unbalance the saddle (and the rider) and – rather than affording protection – bring painful pressure to bear on the horse's back. As a consequence, it was once really commonplace to see horses with open wounds along the withers, trapezius area and on the sides of the vertebrae in the centre of the back. Even now, there are still some older horses who bear the evidence of such injuries in earlier life in the form of pronounced scarring and white marks.

Thankfully, these old 'saddle fitting' processes and their consequences are becoming rarer nowadays, because a large proportion of horse owners are better educated, more aware of the consequences of poorly fitted equipment and anxious to protect the welfare of their horses.

Often, it is the top professionals who lead the way in this respect, not 'because they can afford it' but because attention to detail is part and parcel of their approach. At the beginning of the recent eventing season, I was called in by a nationally famous rider to check all of his horse's saddles. A few months later, midway through the season, I returned to make further fitting checks and was not surprised to find that several of the horses had changed shape considerably in the interim. This particular rider understands that getting the best out of each horse depends not simply on sheer riding ability, but also on paying attention to every single factor that can affect the well-being of his horses.

Nevertheless, despite increasing enlightenment, there are odd pockets of resistance where the old practices persist. Sometimes, these have a geographical element. Some horse owners are a very long distance from the nearest saddlery business – in some parts of the globe, perhaps hundreds of miles. Under these circumstances, when it is totally impractical for a professional to come and fit a saddle, owners will usually place mail orders. However, in such cases, a good deal of use can be made of modern means of communication. For example, photos and templates can be sent to the distant saddler to give at least a reasonable indication of the horse's size, shape and musculature. Thus there is at least a good chance that any saddle sent by mail will not be totally inappropriate. It should be stressed, however, that this method of purchasing a saddle is, at best, an expedient for dealing with extreme circumstances – it comes a very poor second to a thorough back assessment and fitting carried out by a qualified professional.

What, then, is the mystery that lies behind saddle fitting? Why do we seek to complicate what appears, to every riding instructor and Pony Club District Commissioner, to be such a simple procedure? Here lies the rub! Far from being a simple procedure, saddle fitting is, in fact, a very complex and involved undertaking.

At this point I should perhaps reiterate my earlier claim that, from the horse's perspective, saddle fitting is an exercise in damage limitation. We have just seen some of the disadvantages of incorrect fitting and it is obvious that the horse can perform far better without any kind of encumbrance strapped to his back – especially if this is compounded by a further encumbrance in the form of an unbalanced rider. Before outlining the criteria that form the foundation of successful fitting, I should point out that there are many new and revolutionary designs of saddle being marketed today – saddles without trees, with half-trees, with detachable panels and so on – but because many of these have not yet been tried and tested over any significant length of time, I intend for the time being to confine my remarks to what is the traditional and well-tried basic design used in ninety-nine per cent of the worlds' saddles.

A saddle is generally a fairly rigid structure, based upon the tree, but this can be more or less flexible depending on its type and construction. The tree is surrounded by a leather panel, seat and flaps, the whole permitting the tree to carry a rider in a given position with some degree of stability, at various speeds and gaits and, where applicable, over jumps. If this is to be done successfully, it is essential that the horse is able to move in the least restrictive manner possible, taking into account the physical constraints placed upon him by not being able to rotate his two scapulae (shoulder blades) fully under some circumstances and carrying a rider of indeterminate weight who may possibly be moving backwards, forwards and to either side. It is indeed fortunate that horses are such obliging creatures and that, given care and consideration, they put up with most things without becoming difficult or mean. However, we are all aware of what is often considered an 'antisocial' or 'difficult' tendency on the part of some horses when being saddled up – or even approached with a saddle or bridle. It is, of course, true that some horses are lazy and don't like to work. But, in most of these cases, it is far more likely that, at some time in the particular horse's history, badly fitting equipment caused pain and restriction of movement and such an animal can hardly be blamed for showing a lack of enthusiasm to be ridden.

The Rider's Requirements

In due course I am going to examine in some detail the suitability of certain types of saddles for specific purposes, but for the moment I intend to generalize. If a saddle permits the rider to sit in the centre of the seat, with the upper and lower leg in what is regarded as the classical position, and permits the rider's body to remain balanced at all times and for the rider to feel secure and comfortable no matter what the horse is doing, this surely is all we can reasonably expect. (One might also think this fairly easy to achieve.) Not so. Why? Riders, as we all know, come in a huge variety of shapes, sizes, weights and dimensions, levels of fitness, co-ordination and athleticism. Some may wish to ride at an international level of eventing and be what many regard as 'complete horsemen', whereas the happy hacker or trail rider wants nothing more than a safe carriage from which to view the scenery and relax. There are simply monumental differences in the fulfilment of these expectations, which we will examine in more detail in due course. It is the job of the saddle fitter, on behalf of the client, to accommodate all of these ambitions and desires, in many cases with a very limited budget. Just imagine the different sorts of saddle that need to be kept in stock to suit animals ranging from a pony of 11.2 hands to a horse of 17.2 hands, with various widths of fitting from extra narrow to extra, extra wide; to be suitable for pleasure riding, showing, dressage, showjumping, cross-country jumping, long distance riding and hunting; for riders ranging from very young children on a leading rein to 6 ft 6 in heavyweights; some riders long between hip and knee, others short; large bottoms, small bottoms – you get the picture. Then there are the personal preferences: deep seats, flat seats, medium seats, large knee rolls, small knee rolls, non-existent knee rolls, large flaps, long flaps and then of course colour; black, brown of several shades, and designer labels.

I hope by now that you can understand the complexity of the job involved in fitting a particular horse with the right saddle for the right discipline of the right colour with the right label on any one particular day. The miracle is that most saddlers get it right most of the time. Occasionally, saddles have to be made to measure or bespoke, but this is certainly not the general rule. Indeed, there is the added complication that when a saddle is made specifically in this way, at the time it is produced the rider has not sat on it and the horse has not yet had the opportunity to move in it, and it is a sad fact that often, when eventually delivered, such saddles do not meet the expectations of the rider when it comes to comfort and feel. By contrast, a saddle that can be found from stock that fulfils all the requirements allows thorough testing by both horse and rider and is more likely to provide lasting satisfaction.

There is no substitute for the benefits of years of training and experience that are available from a Qualified Saddle Fitter and it is not the aim of the following chapters to educate readers to that level. However, I hope that the information will help to dispel old wives' tales and fallacies, point out potential problems and remedies and assist readers to gain a reasonably comprehensive understanding of the main principles. To assist in this, the text contains a number of true anecdotes that illustrate the various technical points made along the way.

Qualifications for Saddle Making and Fitting

Master Saddlers

The title 'master saddler' is much abused and much misunderstood. In the United Kingdom, 'master' has traditionally been regarded as the ultimate title for the craftsman and it seems to me that any reasonable person would expect a master saddler to be an expert with the ability to design, make, fit, alter or repair anything to do with saddlery. Sadly, this is not necessarily so. While the titles Master Saddler and Qualified Saddle Fitter, when awarded by the Society of Master Saddlers, convey very specific status, there is nothing to stop anyone describing themselves as a 'master saddler' should they wish to do so. To complicate the issue further, there are many genuinely expert craftsmen, who are deemed to be master saddlers, who actually know little or nothing about horses and would certainly not be qualified to fit saddles since they have no understanding of horses' conformation, way of going or potential problems. Happily, there are some individuals who are master craftsmen who do have a profound understanding of horses and their ways, and are proficient riders themselves. Plainly, such individuals would be more desirable for attending to all your saddlery needs – particularly so if they are also Qualified Saddle Fitters.

Qualified Saddle Fitters

A Qualified Saddle Fitter may, or may not be, a working craft saddler, but certainly needs to have a proficient understanding of the methods by which saddles are constructed, and of what alterations could be made to suit various horses' problems of conformation. Thus, while desirable, it is not absolutely necessary for a Qualified Saddle Fitter to be able to work on a saddle personally. It is, however, absolutely essential that such a person has a comprehensive knowledge of the horse in general and of breeds, sizes and the requirements of the various riding disciplines and it is my experience that the best saddle fitters do ride themselves. (Because of this distinction between saddle making and saddle fitting, my comments in the following chapters regarding the construction and design of saddles will be confined to those aspects which must be part and parcel of a saddle fitter's knowledge and experience. Thus, no attempt will be made to go into the considerable, intricate detail that would be necessary in a text book on saddle construction.)

In the United Kingdom, in order to become a Qualified Saddle Fitter, it is necessary to attend the very comprehensive saddle fitting course organized by the Society of Master Saddlers and then undergo an exceedingly rigorous assessment. Successful students are then awarded the 'Qualified' status. Applicants cannot attend the fitting course and assessment until they first have a minimum of three years experience of fitting saddles 'in the field' under the supervision of a qualified member of the Society, and the applicants must, themselves, be members. Once having qualified, in order to maintain their names on the register they must attend a refresher course and seminar every two years. This requirement is intended to maintain a high standard of competence and to keep Qualified Saddle Fitters up to date with all new developments.

Every year the Society of Master Saddlers runs an additional Qualified Saddle Fitters' course for students from overseas. The training requirements and standards of assessment are identical to those of UK applicants and this course is always very well attended by students from all over the world.

All fully qualified Saddle Fitters registered with the Society of Master Saddlers subscribe to and comply with a rigid code of conduct. This guarantees a high level of competence and integrity, coupled with a disciplined operating procedure and the highest business ethics. In addition to this, a thorough complaints procedure should ensure absolute customer satisfaction in the unlikely event of a dispute.

Certified Saddle Fitters

This is a qualification obtained in the United States of America from the Master Saddlers of America. The training is carried out in a similar manner to that of Qualified Saddle Fitter in the United Kingdom, producing excellent standards of competence and experience.

Foundation Course

In addition to the course aimed at producing Qualified Saddle Fitters, there is also a foundation course, a much lower level course in saddle fitting run by the Society of Master Saddlers, which teaches applicants the basics. While this should never be confused with the full Qualified Saddle Fitter designation, it can certainly be regarded as a stepping stone towards it. This course is open to members of the British Equestrian Trade Association (BETA), qualified riding instructors and other equestrian professionals such a physiotherapists, etc.

CHAPTER 1

General Structure of the Saddle

As mentioned in the Introduction, in order for any saddle of any type to be satisfactory, it must fit in such a manner as to permit the horse to move at all gaits and speeds without causing any short- or long-term discomfort or injury. While there are many factors to consider in ensuring that this fundamental criterion is met, the first and most basic is that the tree (effectively the 'chassis' of the saddle) should be appropriate for the horse and the purpose(s) at hand.

The Tree

Almost all saddles are built on a tree of one sort or other. The traditional saddle tree has, for hundreds of years, been made of wood and steel and its basic shape has changed very little (see photos 1 and 2). Nowadays, although many manufacturers still use these well tried and tested materials and designs, it is becoming ever more common to use immensely strong synthetic materials – plastics and polymers – some with and some without steel supports. We will look at these materials, and the options they offer to manufacturers, under the heading Innovations in Tree Design. Whatever the type of construction and materials used, the tree is without question the most important single item in defining the design and character of a saddle, and trees come in a huge variety of styles, sizes and fittings.

Stirrup Bars

Attached to the tree or, in some instances, built into the tree, are the stirrup bars. These can be long, short or adjustable. Extended bars are used for dressage saddles. These allow the stirrup leathers themselves to be positioned further back under the rider's seat, making it easier for their legs to hang in what is considered the classical position. In contrast, jumping saddles often have shorter bars, allowing the leg

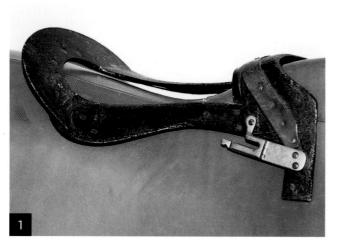

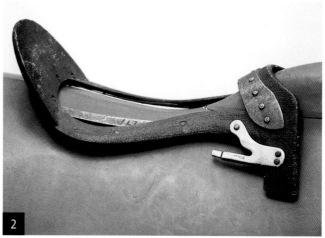

1. A traditional rigid saddle tree of laminated wood with a steel head and gullet plates. An extra strong plate is fitted behind the normal plates to provide additional strength.

2. A Conventional style traditional saddle tree constructed of laminated wood with steel head and gullet plate. This example is a spring tree – note the spring steel strips along its length.

position to be a little forward and, as you would expect, adjustable bars permit the rider to select where they would like the stirrup leathers to hang in relation to their seat bones (see photos 3 and 4). There are also several different types of variable length stirrup bars, which permit the leathers to hang from up to four different positions on a long bar. On some Continental saddles this is facilitated by a slot in the side of the tree to avoid the bulk of a long steel bar under the rider's leg. These systems can vary the location of the stirrup leather by as much as four inches.

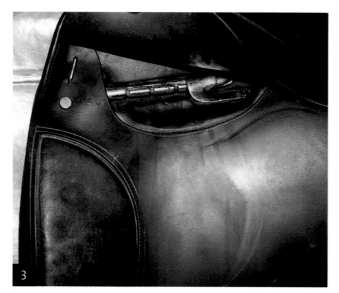

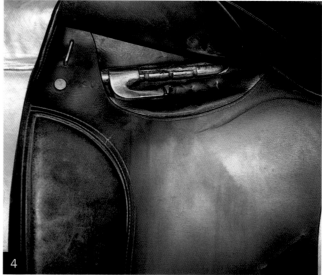

3. Adjustable stirrup bar in rear position – often used to allow for longer leg position.

4. Adjustable stirrup bar in forward position – often used for rider with shorter leathers, as when jumping or doing fast work.

Innovations in Tree Design

I try to remain open-minded to all innovations but I remember with considerable anguish how I welcomed with open arms the advent of the fibreglass tree about twenty years ago. This was so strong that, as a marketing exercise, cars were driven over it to show the strength of the arch. However, approximately five years later – to my considerable pain and embarrassment – these saddles started to snap across the arch in their dozens, and continued to do so. One never sees this type of saddle nowadays as, from the many hundreds sold, the vast proportion failed and this system was consigned to the 'delete box' of history. Thus, while I broadly welcome new materials and other innovations, my enthusiasm is tempered by this lesson from the past. It is probably fair to say, in fact, that the saddle industry as a whole is rather wary of new ideas and perhaps, in some cases, lacks generosity towards them. However, as we shall see from looking at some recent developments in tree design, this does not mean that innovation is rejected out of hand.

Adjustable Trees

Nowadays, some of the more advanced designs of tree permit the width fitting to be changed without disassembling the saddle. The synthetic trees with no metal-work in the head apart from the stirrup bars (that is, those without head or gullet plates – see photos 5 and 6) can be adjusted for various fittings from narrow to extra wide by use of a tree adjuster (see photos 7–11). The saddle is mounted and held square in an engineering jig, heated with heat lamps for a prescribed time, then the required adjustment is made with a very precise widening or narrowing mechanism. The tree is then held in position for several hours whilst it cools, after which the new fitting will be maintained.

This particular system has been used for a number of years now, with tremendous success. These trees are tremendously strong and have another significant advantage over their wood and metal counterparts in that, when the saddle is placed upon the horse, girthed and loaded, it will retain its predetermined angle

5 and 6. A superior make of synthetic saddle tree with no metal gullet or head plate, permitting a huge amount of fitting adjustment for saddlers with the correct jig equipment. These trees are immensely strong and reliable: I have fitted many hundreds of this type over the years and have never had one break.

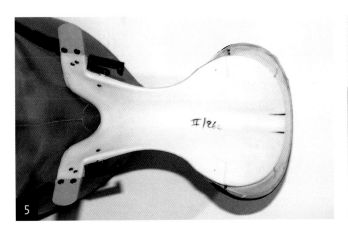

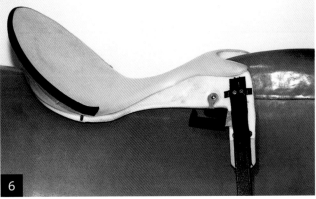

for a few minutes but then gradually open by about 0.6 of an inch. This, we regard as its datum line, and as the horse's scapulae rotate, the tree will move in harmony with the shoulders. This permits the horse to move very freely and indeed, often much more freely than a similar saddle with a rigid metal head and gullet plate in the tree. This is particularly noticeable in lengthened and extended trot and in downward transitions (see Photo 12). Many horses with large shoulder movement perform really well upon changing to a saddle of this type.

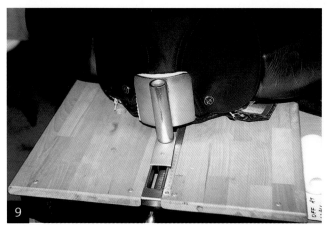

7–11. Series showing the jig and equipment used for adjusting synthetic trees.

12. Downward transition from canter to trot showing free extension of the horse's forearm, indicating comfortable front fitting of the saddle tree and panel but rear of panel lifting slightly.

It should be noted, however, that *adjustments to this type of tree must NEVER be undertaken without the proper equipment and substantial training and understanding of* the system. Stories are legion of amateurs attempting alterations of this sort with hairdryers and an engineering vice and ending up with crooked and malformed trees and injured horses.

Adjustable Gullet Plates

Other modern designs of saddle that do incorporate head and/or gullet plates may still allow the width fitting to be altered by the simple expedient of moving the plate(s) through a variety of angles, ranging from narrow to extra wide (see photos 13 and 14). Again, these trees often afford some degree of flexibility across the points, permitting the horse's scapulae to rotate more freely than trees of traditional construction.

In such designs, adjustments and readjustments can be made in minutes. Since the actual altering of the gullet plate to a wider or narrower fitting requires very few tools and no great skill, this job can be, and often is, undertaken by the owner. However, what does require significant skill is choosing which gullet plate to use for which horse. Furthermore, the effect of changing this plate on the fit of the rest of the panel needs to be understood, as the width of the tree at the front is only one factor in the seven points of saddle fitting (see Chapter 3). In my view, therefore, this apparently simple adjustment is best undertaken by a Qualified Saddle

13. Panel fixed by two bolts and Velcro; gullet plates fixed to tree with two bolts.

14. Colour-coded interchangeable gullet plates – different colours denote different widths.

Fitter. At the very least, it should not be contemplated or undertaken without considerable thought and care and should be overseen by someone with thorough knowledge of all of the points of saddle fitting. The old saying 'a little knowledge is a dangerous thing' is highly appropriate here.

The Tri-form Tree

At the time of writing, a new and exciting saddle tree concept has just been released onto the market (see photo 15). It is described by the manufacturers as the 'ultimate saddle fitting solution' and the biggest step forward since the creation of the saddle tree. A proud and ambitious boast, you might think. However, I have examined this new tree very carefully. It is very well researched, beautifully made and – if it indeed lives up to expectations – I for one will welcome it with open arms. Again, I quote the makers:

> The tri-form tree is a unique engineering concept in which the head of the saddle tree is completely independent from the seat, allowing alternative head profiles to be fitted either at the time of manufacture or at the site of saddle fit. This unique system offers a flexibility and accuracy that has never been seen before and has only been made possible due to recent advancements in software development and engineering technology, using manufacturing techniques and materials more commonly found in the industries of aerospace and Formula 1 motor racing.

This tree is being tested in many different types of saddle. There are five different head fittings, three seat sizes and three cantles and these can be assembled in any combination in a matter of minutes. From the saddle fitting perspective the heads can be changed on site in about twenty minutes. By virtue of the saddler holding a range of tri-form heads, any one saddle can be adjusted to one of five fittings without the need for the saddle to be sent back to the manufacturer for adjust-

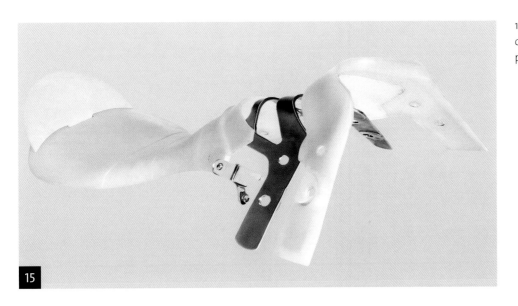

15. The new Tri-form tree that is currently undergoing active practical trials.

ment. In my opinion, the real key to the success of this product will lie in how many different manufacturers will be prepared to change their construction routines – a factor that is not easy to predict.

The Western Tree

In the United States, Western saddles have, for generations, been made on wooden trees, often covered with cheesecloth or canvas, sometimes with rawhide (of which the best quality is called 'bullhide'). Like all handmade products, this type of construction sometimes lacks symmetry. It is probably true to say that the majority of Western saddles are now made on synthetic trees, which come in literally dozens of different shapes, sizes and types depending on their precise intended purpose (see next chapter). One of the synthetic materials used is fibreglass, but I have not heard of this causing the problems in Western Saddles that were associated with English saddles in times past, as described earlier in this chapter.

The Western tree has three major components: the swell, the cantle and the bars. (Note that, in Western saddles, 'bars' does not refer to stirrup bars, but to major structures that run from front to rear of the saddle, either side of the horse's spine.) Additionally, there are variations in the shape of horn, gullet and swell width (see photos 64–6 in Chapter 2).

The Seat

Traditionally, the manufacturing saddler would take a bare tree and 'prepare' it. This meant that webbings would be stretched lengthways and crossways and the foam seat would be shaped and fitted so that the leather seat and skirts could be

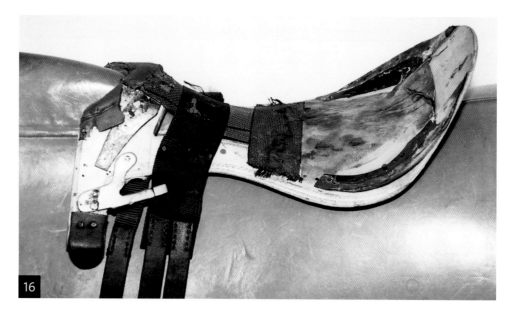

16

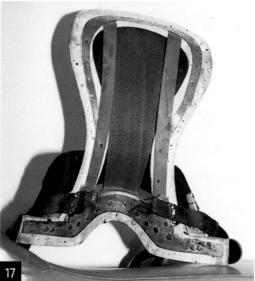

17

Preparing the seat.
16 and 17. Stretching the webbing lengthways and crossways.

16. Shows the tree having had the foam seat removed exposing top side of webbings. This photo and 17 show stretching the webbing lengthways and crossways. 17 also shows a missing rivet on the gullet plate and the attachment of the foremost billet strap.

18. The basic seat in place. Note that the tree used here for illustration purposes is of poor quality, made with very thin wood laminates and with the metal head and gullet plates left unfinished and unprotected.

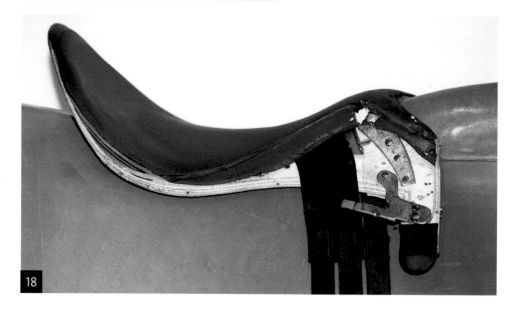

18

added (see photos 16, 17 and 18). It is becoming increasingly common with the modern, synthetic trees for much of this work to be done during the moulding of the tree, thus requiring the manufacturing saddler just to add the covering seat and skirts. I use the phrase 'just to add' rather than 'simply to add', because this job is far from simple and has always required considerable experience. However, one cannot help noticing that the traditional saddlers' skills are being gradually superseded by modern scientific techniques and production line operations – the moulding of trees being one example.

The Panel

The panel is the 'envelope' between the tree and the horse which contains either flocking material ('stuffing' of wool, felt or synthetic material – see photo 19) or air cushioning, or is pre-formed of synthetic material, or is a mixture of all of these elements. It is simply the method of sustaining the rider's weight over the horse's back and spreading this weight over as large an area as possible while still allowing the horse to move freely. Plainly, as a physical principle, the greater the area of the panel, the fewer pounds per square inch of the rider's weight are transmitted to the horse's back, and this reduces the possibility of trauma and bruising. However, there are practical limitations as to how large the panel can be, dictated by equine conformation in general and, on certain individuals, further constraints may be imposed by individual conformation – for example, a short back.

There is now on the market a saddle designed with a significantly variable panel – see The Variable Panel Saddle in Chapter 2.

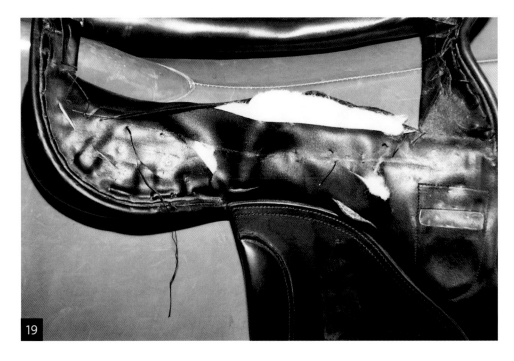

19. A traditional flock-filled panel opened up to show flocking and flocking slots.

The Use of Air in Panels

Before discussing conventional flocking and issues related to re-flocking in detail, let us look at past and current attempts to use air an as alternative 'filling' for panels.

Panels filled with air as opposed to flocking material are by no means a new idea. Indeed, the concept is a very old one, first tried in Germany in the early years of the twentieth century. However, until fairly recently, there has been a major problem of reliability. Generally speaking, the way in which the system operates is by the placing of airbags within the leather panel (see photo 20). These bags can be either inflatable for adjustment, or sealed units. With the latter, there is often also some flocking within the panel to allow for some level of adjustment. When the system works well, it can have tremendously beneficial results as it eliminates lumps, ridges and unevenness. Patently, no matter how unevenly the saddle itself is weighted, the pounds pressure is absolutely even throughout the length of the bag. Depending upon the inflation pressure in the first instance, it is also, to some degree, self-adjusting.

20. A transparent demonstration panel showing air bag (black) and flocking (white).

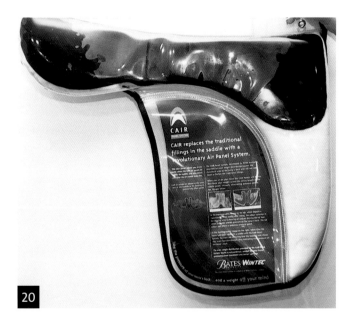

Despite this attractive principle, in practice, the system has frequently had its drawbacks. A few years ago, an enthusiastic manufacturer produced an air system which featured an air panel made up of more than one bag and, if these bags were not very carefully placed in the panel, one could feel a ridge along the joining areas. Also, the earlier designs used air valves which could be inflated whilst on the horse (see photo 21). These were fairly large and not cosmetically attractive and, in day-to-day use, a few of these valves started to leak, causing some panel deflation. While this only happened in a small percentage of cases, sadly this product did suffer a loss of reputation among some of the supplying saddlers and clients.

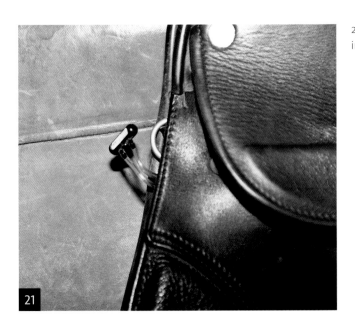

21. Air valve with inflation tube.

However, the product is now much improved with smaller and neater valves and is far less prone to deflation problems.

Another disadvantage of adjustable air bag systems in general is that, left to the untrained individual, the panels were often over-inflated, which tended to make the saddles bounce rather like an over-inflated Lilo. It takes considerable skill to adjust the panel to the correct pressure based upon the horse's conformation and the size and the weight of the rider. This system does, however, have a substantial advantage over a conventional panel when employed by an experienced fitter to accommodate an asymmetrical horse. We will look at the problems posed by asymmetry further in due course (see Chapter 4) but, basically, if one shoulder is larger than the other, the movement of the larger shoulder will tend to push the conventionally flocked panel away from the movement and the whole saddle will move across to a greater or lesser degree. With an air-filled panel, the air simply moves back away from the shoulder for that brief moment and then returns in synchronization with the movement of the horse. Thus, in practice, the saddle movement is minimized. In addition to this, I have noticed that horses with historically sore or tender backs have benefited enormously from air-filled panels, particularly when ridden by heavy or poorly balanced riders.

Air-filled panels are now available factory-fitted from some manufacturers. Alternatively, they can be fitted to an existing saddle by a skilled Master Saddler as these air bags come in a variety of sizes and shapes to suit most production saddles for all disciplines.

A modified form of the air-filled panel is the semi-filled panel. This employs a sealed air bag which cannot be adjusted and is statistically less likely to suffer deflation than the inflatable type as it has no working parts. This type of panel is often partially flocked and partially air-filled and the makers claim that small adjustments can be made quite satisfactorily to the flocked section of the panel while still retaining evenness of pressure because of the presence of the air bag. I have seen very impressive scientific studies and illustrations of this particular product and, as yet, have not heard of a single failure or depressurization.

Flocking and Re-flocking

The traditional flocking or panel-filling materials are wool or felt, with modern forms being either a wool/synthetic mix or entirely synthetic. For various reasons, the most common being settlement through wear and changes to the horse's shape, saddles sometimes need re-flocking. The specific reasons for re-flocking will be dealt with in more detail as they arise but, for the time being, I would like to discuss some issues that relate to the general process. I find that these turn up time and again and they obviously continue to create confusion. The following is a letter from a client (reproduced with her permission) which serves to highlight some of these issues.

> When my saddle needed re-flocking your saddler came and re-flocked it on the spot. She then refitted it, made further adjustments and finally refitted it again. I have been very pleased with the results, my horse is going well, his back is swinging and he is obviously very comfortable.
>
> Recently a client's saddle needed re-flocking and, to my surprise her saddler took it away to do the work. A couple of days later he rang up, told her the work was finished, and asked her to collect it from the shop. The saddle wasn't refitted and to me it seemed to have been over-flocked; it is quite hard and the horse has rubbed – never having done so previously – on both sides corresponding with the back of the saddle. I also noticed the saddle is tending to bounce.
>
> I am a full-time instructor and so, although my knowledge about saddles is limited, my eye is tuned to notice the sort of things I am describing! I have suggested the client contacts the saddler and asks him to examine the problem – but so far he has not responded.

Opinions differ as to whether saddles should be re-flocked at the client's premises and fitted to the horse's back to perfection, or removed and the work undertaken on the bench at the workshop. As the writer of this letter is aware, my own preference is for the former and my saddlers almost always carry out such work at the client's premises, which makes it easier to refit the saddle – and also eliminates the possibility of the client being without it, possibly for several days. When the work is undertaken in the workshop, the saddler will be required to make a return journey, involving mileage and time expenses and the client should be prepared to pay for this service in much the same way as paying for other 'second visits'. However, key points about re-flocking, regardless of where it is done, are first, that the saddle should be re-flocked to suit the back profile of the individual horse and second, that the saddle should be properly refitted afterwards.

Another misunderstanding sometimes arises amongst horse owners who expect their saddles to be re-flocked until very firm to the point of hardness! Flocking is intending to 'cushion' and reduce trauma. If the saddle is over-flocked it will be hard, the cushioning properties will be lost, pressure points may be created and the horse is likely to become sensitive and may be rubbed and bruised.

The letter writer mentions that her client's saddle is tending to bounce. This is likely to be because it has been over-flocked and it is this movement that is creating 'rubs' on the horse's back. Bouncing is also often the result of too much flocking in the centre of the panel.

After I received this letter I rang the writer and discussed how she could persuade her client to obtain better advice and I am pleased to report that the problem was subsequently resolved.

It can be very difficult for horse owners to recognize when their saddle requires re-flocking. However, as a rule of thumb, the fitting of the saddle should be checked at least once a year; my preference is for every six months and more regularly if, for any reason, the horse undergoes changes in shape. In addition to the obvious causes – a long period off work, a hard season, the maturing and ageing processes – it should be noted that horses can undergo change of shape in terms of developing asymmetrically. The various causes of this problem are discussed further in Saddle Moving to One Side (in Chapter 4), but addressing it usually involves adjusting the saddle's flocking, amongst other measures.

When the fitting of a saddle is checked using the services of a Society of Master Saddlers Qualified Saddle Fitter, the saddle fitter will recommend any adjustments necessary, whatever their cause. While small adjustments can be achieved adequately without dropping the entire panel, the purist will always prefer to replace all the flocking, necessitating complete panel removal. Make no mistake, re-flocking demands considerable skill and should only be undertaken by a genuinely skilled and preferably qualified practitioner. In just the same way, the saddle should have originally been fitted by a Qualified Saddle Fitter who, as we have seen, will have undergone rigorous assessment in order to qualify and is bound by a strict code of conduct.

The Saddle Flap

The saddle flap must be cut and formed as appropriate to the particular discipline for which the saddle is to be used. For instance, the dressage saddle will be cut very straight, with a long, narrow flap to permit the rider to sit with a long, fairly straight leg position (see photo 22). The jumping saddle will have a shorter, forward-cut flap to enable the rider to adopt a jumping position (see photo 23) and the general purpose saddle will have a flap and panel design which, hopefully, will permit the rider to participate in many different disciplines with the same saddle.

22. Dressage saddle.

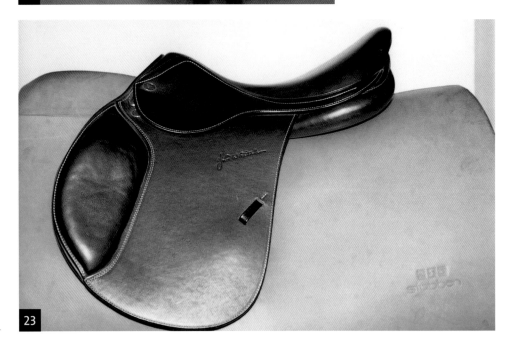

23. Jumping saddle.

The Girth or Billet Straps

When constructing a saddle it is often mechanically convenient to have the billet straps mounted on webbings in approximately the centre of the panel. However, of late it is becoming more frequent to see the use of point and balance straps formed in the position of a yoke (see photos 24 and 25). This method has a number of advantages. The front or point strap often stops the saddle moving forward on a horse during downward transitions, a fact that is most often found to be advantageous when saddling types such as Cobs, Arabs, and Quarter Horses, and the rear balance strap often prevents saddles from bouncing up and down at the back of the panel and the cantle swinging from side to side. All of these issues will be examined in detail in due course.

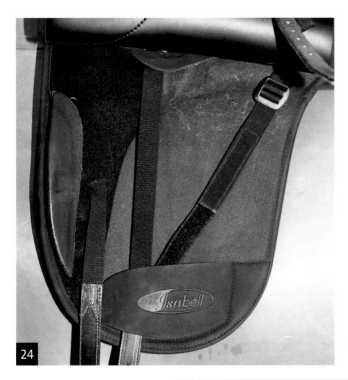

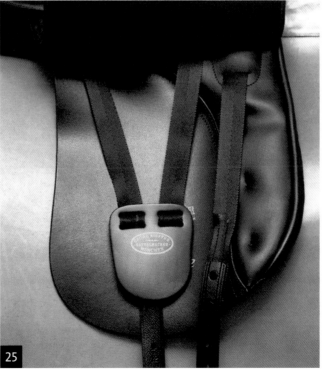

24 and 25. Yoke arrangements of girth straps on dressage saddles.

Advantages and Disadvantages of Natural and Synthetic Materials

As we have seen, for hundreds of years, saddles were constructed from the same materials – wood and metal, various types of leather and wool. Beautifully crafted traditional saddles made of these materials are still available but the use of synthetic materials, mainly plastics and polymers, is increasingly common and it is no longer true to describe entirely synthetic saddles as 'cheap and nasty'. Some of the very best designs, constructed primarily of synthetics, are used even at the highest level of competition.

Wherever a choice exists in materials and design, there are always advantages and disadvantages to be considered. Those pertaining to saddle construction can be summarized as follows.

Natural Materials

Advantages of totally traditional construction and the certain knowledge that, if properly cared for, the saddle will last a lifetime and will always retain its aesthetic beauty – plus the financial incentive of a high second-hand resale value.

Disadvantages are a high initial investment and the necessity of caring for the leather in an appropriate manner.

Synthetic Materials

Advantages are that they are immensely strong, hardly affected by moisture and heat and do not rot. Saddles made of these materials are a less expensive initial outlay and are often very comfortable when new.

Disadvantages are that they can be cosmetically unappealing, especially after considerable use and have a very low resale value. Also, in most cases, we don't yet know how well these materials will wear and continue to give good service in the very long term. I have previously mentioned the example of the fibreglass trees which, initially and under certain loadings, appeared to be very strong, yet started snapping across the arch in great quantity within five years of use. Despite its many undoubted qualities and uses, the material simply had not been tested in this context over a long period, and when it was used for this purpose, it turned out to be unsuitable.

While we only move forward by exploring innovations, it should be remembered that a saddle is a very specific piece of equipment, traditionally expected to last 'a lifetime' (and certainly twenty to twenty-five years) and many of the new materials have simply not been around that long to date. It cannot and should not be inferred from the fibreglass experience that other synthetic materials will fail in time, but it is a fact that many have yet to stand the test of time to which traditional materials have long been subjected.

Further to this, there have been many reports that the girth straps on synthetic saddles, whilst very strong in terms of tensile strength, are prone to tearing around the punched holes, and this is something that users should keep a check on. Some people, in fact, have been known to have the synthetic straps replaced with leather.

CHAPTER 2

Types of Saddle

The General Purpose Saddle

The general purpose saddle, all-purpose saddle and event saddle are different names for the same thing – a saddle that tries to be all things to all people and thus a compromise; a saddle that will allow one to ride adequately whether working on the flat, jumping a fence or hacking.

Many people who own a horse will have one saddle for all purposes and the choice will almost always be a saddle of this type. Patently, the saddle has to fit the horse properly whatever its type and description, but the specification of a general purpose saddle will place a greater responsibility on the saddle fitter to establish which type of riding is the most important to the particular client. If, for example, the client is a person who likes to participate in many types of Riding Club activities (anything from showjumping to dressage) the saddle fitter will be taking particular note of the rider's shape and size. One of the primary considerations will be the length of leg from point of hip to point of knee.

If the general purpose saddle is to fulfil its role adequately, when the rider is sitting in the centre of the saddle, in the correct position, it should be possible for them to adopt a long, fairly classical leg position for work on the flat without the top of the long boot interfering with the bottom of the saddle flap – or, indeed, the leg coming off the back of the flap. Additionally, if the rider then shortens the stirrup leathers for jumping, the knee must not come above the knee roll, or come off the front of the flap. This is the kind of general purpose saddle which should allow the rider to participate adequately in, let us say, Riding Club eventing.

The General Purpose VSD Saddle

The initials VSD are an abbreviated form of a German phrase meaning 'dressage/all-purpose'. Since all of the photos 26–29 are of VSD saddles, one might expect them to look pretty much the same. Plainly, they do not – it is sadly the case that, in the saddle industry, labels and names can be rather misleading. Such saddles should, in theory, be quite straight-cut with a fairly long flap, permitting the rider to work with a long, classical leg position but also to have the facility to shorten the stirrup leathers in order to jump small fences.

Generally speaking, most VSD saddles will have a medium to deep seat, and a flap which is cut straight enough so as not to interfere with the horse's shoulder movement and is also long enough so that its bottom edges will not interfere with the tops of the rider's long boots when the rider has adopted a suitable flatwork leg position. Usually a VSD saddle will not have thigh rolls and the knee rolls will tend

26–29. Various patterns of general purpose VSD saddles.

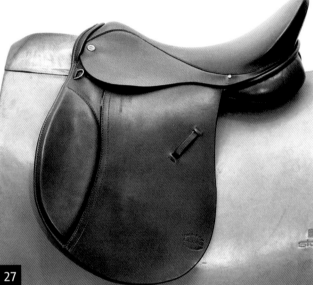

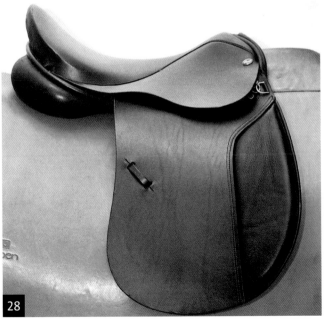

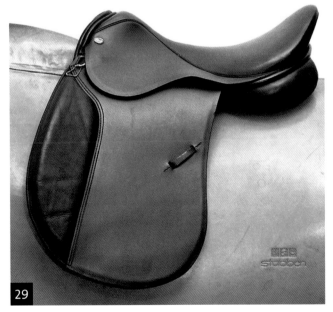

to be of fairly modest size. Many VSD saddles will have extra long stirrup bars of the type associated with pure dressage saddles to accommodate the longer leg position.

Saddles of this type, especially those in wider fittings and/or for horses with large shoulders, will often be fitted with a point and balance strap, forming a yoke, which tends to stop a saddle moving forward and the rear panel being 'overactive'.

This type of general purpose saddle can best be described as a 'dressage all purpose saddle'. It assumes that the rider's primary interest is in working on the flat, with only a small amount of jumping, and that not over large fences. Since it has a long flap, almost vertically cut at the back and not very forward-cut over the shoulder, one often sees this type of saddle used in various lower-level showing classes and Working Hunter classes.

The Jumping General Purpose Saddle

As the name suggests, this would be the choice of the rider whose prime interest is jumping, with just a little work on the flat. This type of saddle will be a little more forward-cut than the VSD, and the line of the saddle flap will also be more forward, not allowing the lower leg to come back to the classical position for flat-work (see photos 30–33). Also, the flap itself would not be as long as in the VSD. The under-panel may well have thigh rolls, encouraging the rider's legs into a more forward position. Often, in the more modern designs, there will be no knee rolls as such but small rolls or 'lumps' which sits above the knees, permitting the rider to shorten the stirrup leathers significantly while still being able to remain sitting in the centre of the saddle. (In some of the older designs, a rider with long thighs would have to put their knees behind the knee rolls and, by doing so, would tend to sit too far back in the saddle.)

In the search to design the most comprehensive general purpose saddles, many manufacturers have employed imaginative design features. One of the better known English manufacturers has a system of changeable knee pads mounted on thick Velcro strips and secured by press studs at the top and bottom (see photos 34–36). There are three types of knee pad: jumping, general purpose and dressage. These pads take literally only a few seconds to change. This is a very clever idea which has found wide approval among riders of all abilities.

Another system made in Great Britain, by an American-owned company, employs a flap which pivots at the back and has an adjustable plate at the front to give varying degrees of angle over the shoulder.

I have seen many similar designs incorporating a variable length of stirrup bars and/or completely changeable flaps, but both of the systems mentioned have been in production successfully for many years.

In conclusion, the general purpose/all-purpose/event saddle is a compromise which attempts to be all things to all riders with varying degrees of success. These saddles are made by most of the world's manufacturers in various colours, styles,

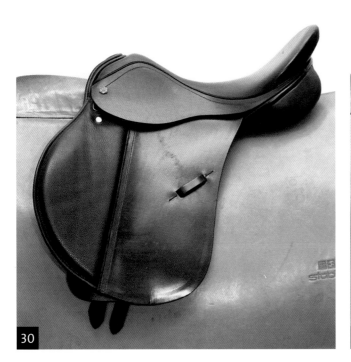

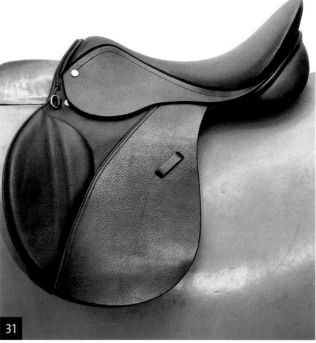

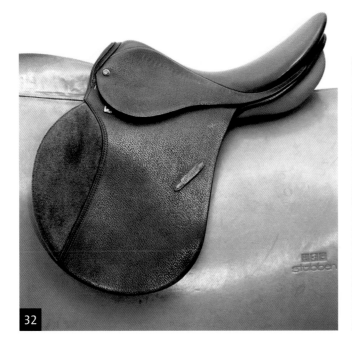

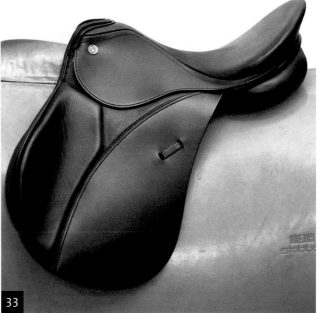

30–33. Various patterns of jumping general purpose saddle.

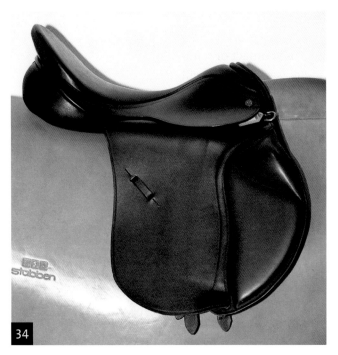

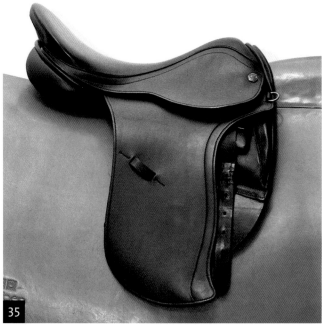

34–36. The design features of the saddle with changeable knee pads.

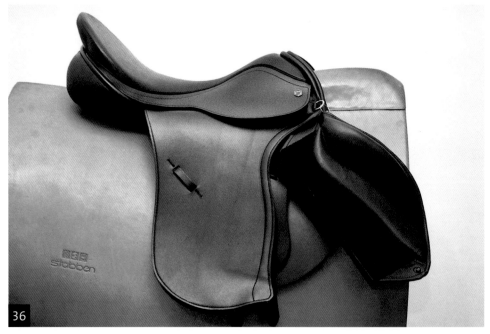

leather qualities and types, with a huge range of prices. So, before your saddle fitter attends with a large selection, remember that (aside from an accurate description of the horse and a realistic guide to the purchaser's budget) the crucial information required of the rider will be height, weight, length from point of hip to point of knee and as precise an explanation as possible of the type of riding you favour. Saddles can then be selected to limit your choice to those that are likely to suit you best. All these points will be explored further in the next chapter.

The Jumping Saddle

Most serious jumping riders throughout the world now use close-contact or semi-close-contact saddles. Generally speaking, close-contact saddles (see photo 37) will have a flat or shallow seat with a square cantle and either a very thin or fairly thin panel moulded from a polymer mix or felt (see photo 38), permitting the rider's legs to feel, and indeed be, in close contact to the horse. The semi-close-contact saddle (see photos 39 and 40) will look fairly similar but will have a flocked panel of wool or synthetic/wool mix in the traditional manner (see photo 41) and will thus be adjustable to a reasonable extent – this is generally not possible with the genuine close-contact saddle, which accommodates only minimal adjustment.

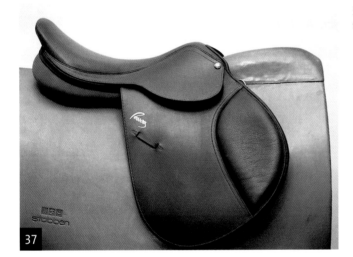

37. A close-contact jumping saddle.

38. Moulded panel of a close-contact saddle.

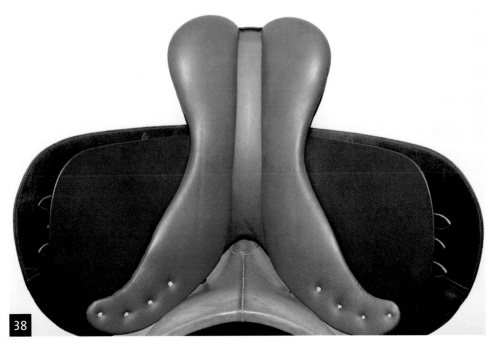

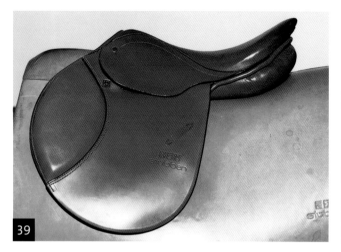

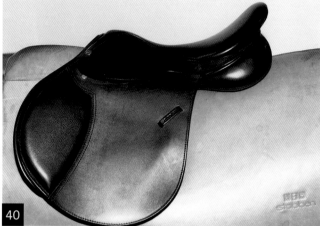

39 and 40. Two examples of semi-close-contact saddles.

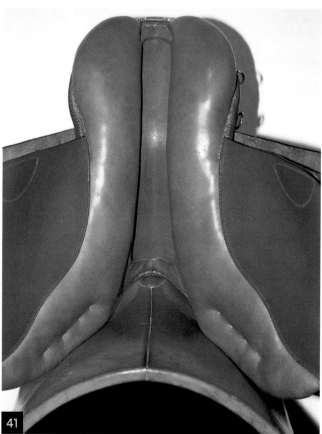

41. The flocked panel of a semi-close-contact saddle.

Initially, most riders find using a close-contact saddle rather more difficult than a conventional jumping saddle with deep seat, large rolls, etc. However, in my experience, once they have practised on and become familiar with the close-contact model, few want to revert to the older design.

The close-contact saddle can best be characterized not by what it does for the rider, but by what it does not do when the rider gets the striding wrong, particularly in combination fences. The shallow seat of the close-contact saddle gives the rider the ability to use the upper body with considerable freedom to counter-balance rapidly should the horse put in an especially long or short stride, whereas with the more deep-seated saddle the rider is more 'wedged in'; this is fine when all goes well but, if the horse has to make an extraordinary effort, an inexperienced rider is likely to be catapulted into an unbalanced position by the cantle of the saddle.

The Dressage Saddle

Dressage presupposes that the rider will want to ride in what is normally regarded, worldwide, as the classical position. This implies that the rider will be in complete balance, sitting on the seat bones in the centre of the saddle with a long leg posi-tion. Looking at a rider, one would anticipate a vertical line between the ankle, hip and shoulder. Most serious riders would hope to achieve this balanced and elegant position and they can be aided significantly by a saddle that is designed for the specific purpose (see photos 42–44). There are hundreds of dressage designs, of which I have illustrated only three, but they almost always have the following fea-tures: a medium to deep seat, a long, straight-cut flap and stirrup bars mounted far enough back to permit the stirrup leathers to hang vertically virtually under the seat bones (indeed, there are some designs that have adjustable stirrup bars to per-mit five different positions, depending upon the requirements of the rider). Most modern, well-known designs have quite large knee rolls, which may serve to pre-vent riders' legs from coming very far forward – indeed, many riders like the reminder provided by knee rolls in this respect. Further to this, one of the most common comments one hears from dressage instructors to their pupils is, 'Your lower leg is too far forward.' While this may simply be postural error on the rider's part, it may also be induced or exaggerated by the saddle. If it is too high in front or too low behind, it will encourage the rider to sit on the buttocks rather than the

42–44. Three patterns of dressage saddle.

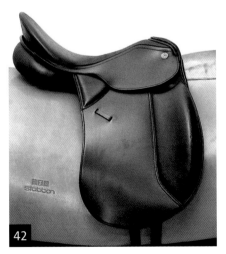

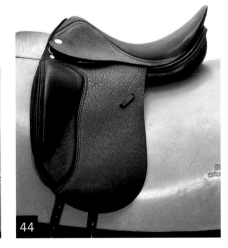

seat bones, which in turn tends to throw the lower leg too far forward. Thus the fitting of a dressage saddle must be undertaken with considerable care.

From the rider's perspective, is also very important to check the length of the saddle flap, as nothing is quite so tiresome as the top edge of a long boot snagging the bottom edge of the saddle flap – which is often a possibility with long-legged riders. Most dressage saddles also have long girth straps and short girths, this arrangement permitting closer contact for the rider's legs, with no buckle bulk beneath them.

Although the fairly deep seat and large knee rolls typify the most popular design of dressage saddle, some very experienced classical riders prefer not to have these features, since they feel that their ability permits them to sit correctly at all times without such physical encouragement.

In respect of fitting the horse, dressage saddles are often easier to fit than jumping or general purpose saddles, especially on horses who have particularly large shoulders, since the panel and flaps will generally sit behind the shoulder and not impede the movement. Most of the modern, well-designed dressage saddles will have some kind of yoke arrangement for the billet straps (see photos 24 and 25, page 21), usually from the points of the tree, with a balance strap as far back as possible. This eliminates any rocking or forward movement, bounce, or lateral swing of the cantle.

Suede or doeskin seats and knee pads, once very popular on dressage saddles, have recently tended to be superseded by very soft hides – buffalo for one – which give superb grip and comfort without becoming 'shiny' or 'shabby'.

The English Showing Saddle

Photos 45–48 are all of English show saddles, so why are they so different? The answer lies in tradition, the specific classes for which they are intended and modern acceptability. Photo 45 shows the most traditional design of show saddle, plain, elegant, flat-seated, square-cantled and almost always brown. Also, note the half-panel shown in photo 49. While this feature is rarely seen nowadays, this is without question the epitome of the traditional English showing saddle. Photos 50 and 51 show working hunter saddles, not quite as vertical in the flap as the traditional showing saddle, often with soft knee pads and almost always with a full panel.

It is surprising how many people nowadays use what is virtually a dressage saddle, with short billet straps and a deep seat, for showing. Indeed, many competitors actually use dressage saddles and cut off the long girth straps. This is not totally acceptable to many judges, particularly when showing at county level or above.

It remains the accepted etiquette for most show classes to present the horse in a brown saddle, although some Native Breed, Arab and Coloured classes find black acceptable.

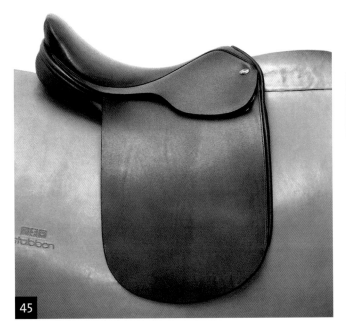

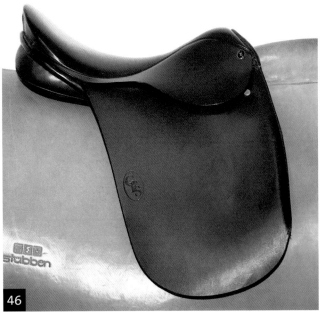

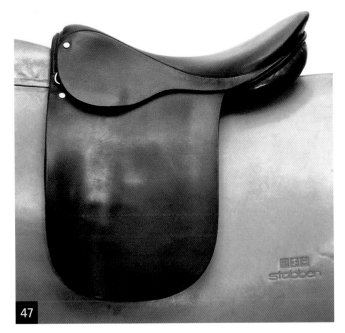

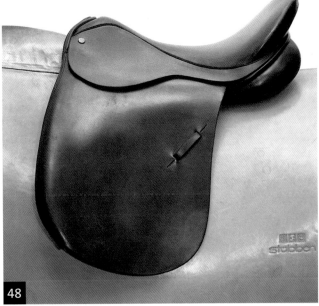

45–48. Four different English showing saddles, of
which the first is the most traditional.

49. The half-panel of a traditional showing saddle.

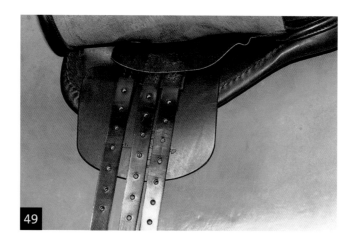

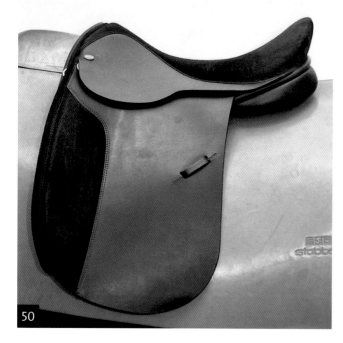

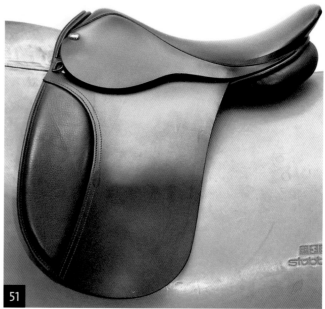

50 and 51. Working hunter saddles.

The Variable Panel Saddle

This is not the actual name of the saddle (I have deliberately not named any manufacturer in this book), but rather a description of what it is supposed to do. Photo 52 shows Sky, a five-year-old Welsh Section D, photo 53 shows him fitted with a variable panel saddle and photo 54 shows the same saddle on a saddle-horse. As can be seen from the photos, the panels (the panel being made in two sections) are very long indeed – sitting well in front of and above the shoulders – and, as can be seen from photos 55 and 56, the panel sections are detachable and are mounted on Velcro-covered rubberized pads at the front and rear. The position of these pads can be altered to change the shape of how the panel lies. The gullet can be widened or made narrower, the panel sections can be further forward or further

52. Sky, a young Welsh Section D.

53. Sky fitted with a variable panel saddle.

54. The variable panel saddle on a saddle-horse.

55 and 56. These two photos of the variable panel saddle show how mounting on Velcro-faced pads can facilitate changing the panel position. Plainly, the panel sections have huge bearing surfaces, but it can be argued that there must be increased pressure under the fixing pads. Some people also regard this system as cosmetically unappealing.

back in relation to the tree and the pads can be of different depths to accommodate different conformation. The panel material itself is very firm, the theory being that, because it is mounted on movable pivots, it can accommodate the changing shape of the horse's back when moving.

I have known this system to work very well on some horses and not at all well on others. I have come across horses, Sky being one, who were significantly sore under the pad locations and because of this did not want to go forward freely. In his case, the answer was to acknowledge that this arrangement did not suit him and to fit a normal panel of a length that did. However, on the positive side, I have known of horses who work very well with this system – but, as always, correct and knowledgeable fitting is the answer.

The Polo Saddle

Two types of polo saddle are shown here. The first (photos 57 and 58) is very traditional, having a medium depth of seat, a close-contact half-panel and a straight head with quite a high rise at the front. This type of tree and panel will often suit the rangy, high-withered polo pony – conformation often associated with this discipline. The particular saddle illustrated has a doeskin seat for extra grip and a completely plain flap, other than the small trim to the front, thus allowing the rider's leg to move more easily if required for tight turns and giving a close feel to the pony. Photo 59 shows a slightly more modern design – again, a medium suede or doeskin seat with a high-rise head, but this particular saddle has a rear gusset and is flocked, enabling the saddle fitter to make significant adjustments to take account of changes in the pony's condition during the season.

It is perhaps not surprising that nowadays polo players often select saddles of a more modern design, usually with a cut back head to make allowance for more prominent withers, and often having a flap with soft pads and rolls. Indeed, it is

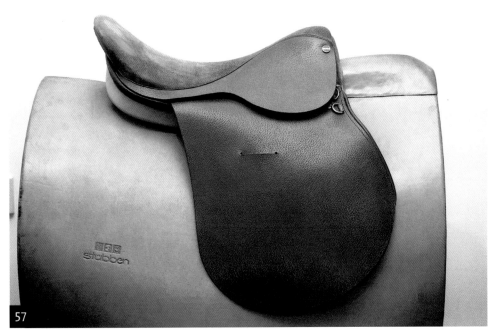

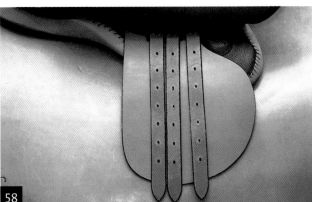

57 and 58. A traditional pattern of polo saddle.

59. A more modern pattern of polo saddle.

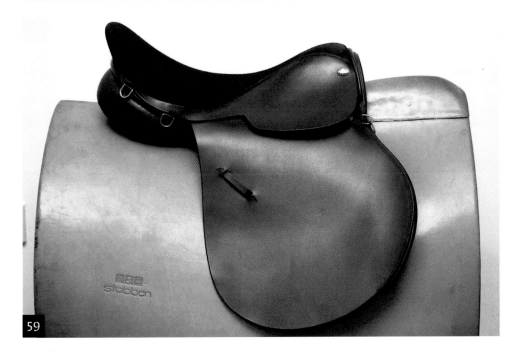

not at all unusual to see polo players riding in Australian stock saddles (described later in this chapter) and similar. Polo is a game that can only be won by scoring goals so performance is valued above style or tradition. However, while it can be a tough and demanding game for both pony and rider, a well-chosen and correctly fitting saddle can add greatly to the performance and comfort of both parties.

The Endurance Saddle

Compared to most other types of saddle, it is not unreasonable to describe the endurance saddle as aesthetically and cosmetically unappealing. The particular example illustrated in photo 60 has a quilted, padded and thus soft seat and skirts, and a soft padded front to the flap, plainly designed for rider comfort. Since many endurance horses are Arabs, Arab crosses or similar types, having short backs, endurance saddles are usually short in length so that the rear panels do not lie on the sensitive lumbar area. It is the nature of this discipline that these generally little horses are ridden over sometimes vast distances in a short time. Their riders can sometimes be technically rather larger than they should be for a short saddle, but their weight has to be distributed evenly to get the least possible pressure per square inch exerted over the entire area of the panel. So, since the horse's conformation dictates that the panel cannot be made longer, it must go wider. The panel in photo 61 is of the non-adjustable, close-contact variety and will never become

60. An endurance saddle.

60

61. A non-adjustable, close-contact panel of an endurance saddle.

lumpy or crease. Note also the width of the gullet, which will permit a saddle cloth to sit inside the gullet and still not rub on each side of the spine if the horse has a raised spine along its length. Despite this feature, it is a fact that various manufacturers of endurance saddles often regard the comfort of the rider as paramount, so the designs are not always as horse-friendly as they might be. This is a point for consideration and discussion with the saddle fitter if you are purchasing a saddle for this discipline.

Recently, a number of people have been using treeless saddles of one sort or another for endurance riding. These do have the advantage of being fairly light but they also have a tendency to move from side to side rather readily, especially on certain body types. For this reason, I have reservations about their suitability for this discipline, especially on rounder barrelled horses.

The Racing Saddle

It has always amazed me that some of the most valuable horses in the world are so badly saddled. There seems to be an ethos in the racing fraternity which says that any saddle will fit any horse, with more or less blankets, rugs, numnahs and saddle cloths under them to disguise the actual fit. Indeed, many jockeys have their own favourite saddle which they take with them to all of their race meetings and put on almost every horse they ride. While some of the reasons for doing this may be questionable (it may be the jockey's 'lucky saddle', but is it lucky for the horse?) others do have some validity. For example, in a sport where riding at the correct weight is crucial, jockeys know the precise weight of their saddles, and have control over the conditions of girths and leathers, which are subjected to considerable stress. However, these issues have nothing to do with the actual conformation of the horse.

Regarding the design of racing saddles there are, of course, two main racing disciplines, flat racing and National Hunt (jump racing). On the flat, horses carry very light weights and, necessarily, the minimalist saddles used are made as light as possible. Over the jumps, the weight range is higher and, when a relatively light jockey is riding a highly weighted horse, there is scope for using a more substantial saddle. Indeed, this option is often favoured, since it makes sense for the prescribed weight to be made up by a saddle that affords the rider greater comfort and security than by the dead weight of lead that has, otherwise, to be carried in the saddle cloth. Whether the bigger saddle is necessarily a good fit for the particular horse is still another question. Point-to-pointing, the amateur version of jump racing, has a number of different races, involving both lady and gentleman riders. The weights carried are relatively high, and some races are open to riders of both genders. It is in these that the biggest variation of saddles may be seen, with some of the larger male riders perched on lightweight 'professional' saddles, while some of the light lady riders will use much more substantial models – some of which may not vary greatly from a very forward-cut jumping saddle.

I have illustrated just two of the many possible designs, a small, lightweight synthetic racing saddle which weighs just a few ounces and a more substantial, traditional 'race exercise' saddle, of the type often used for riding work rather than on the racecourse.

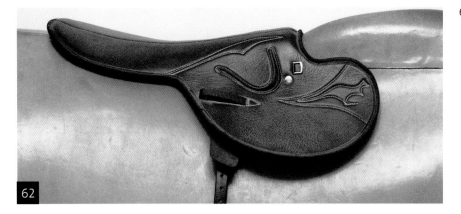

62. A lightweight synthetic racing saddle.

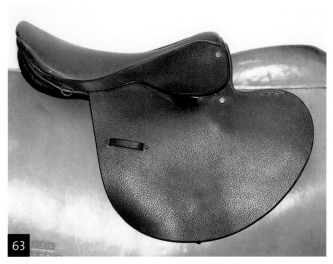

63. A traditional 'race exercise' saddle.

The Western Saddle

The Western saddle comes in many guises, as there are many disciplines of Western riding, such as trail riding, cutting, roping, barrel racing, etc. However, it is not my intention to go into detail about the differences in the saddles for these various disciplines but to concentrate on the most important factor which they have in common – the panel (see photos 64–66). Although the photo sequence actually shows a very small Western saddle, the panel area is huge: even a very small saddle such as this will have a panel area as large, or even larger, than most English saddles of whatever discipline. It is not uncommon, when watching Western films, to see large men on large saddles on what appear to be fairy small Quarter Horses, and in almost all cases the back of the panel will come way beyond the horse's last rib. This would be totally unacceptable with an English-style panel as the horse would almost always become sore in the lower back. But because of the huge bearing surface of the Western saddle the pressure in pounds per square inch is very low and therefore causes no problems whatsoever. What is important, of course, is that the Western saddle should sit in balance; the contour of the tree at the front should still conform to the basic principles and angles which will be described in detail when we discuss the saddle fitting procedure in the next chapter.

One factor which has a considerable impact on the design and fitting of a Western saddle is the shape of the bars. Bar in the Western sense means something completely different from the stirrup bar of European terminology; the Western bars are the structures that run from front to rear in this type of saddle, either side of the horse's spine, joining the fork (front) and cantle (rear) of the saddle. While the bars are usually covered with sheepskin, leather or fabric, there is not the level of protection from them equivalent to the thick, soft, spongy panel of an English saddle. The length and shape of the bars is thus a prime consideration. It relates to the combination described earlier of short-backed breeds carrying fairly heavy riders, requiring a large panel that almost always comes well behind the last rib and covers the lumbar area. To accommodate the short-backed horse, the bars themselves will be flared both font and rear so that no intense pressure is levied on the shoulders or the lumbar regions.

The skirt, covering the bar at the top under the rider's leg, can be a considerable source of pressure and irritation, particularly if the cinch (Western equivalent of the girth) is attached to the skirt rather than the tree. There are three basic ways of attaching the cinch to the saddle, a process that, in Western parlance, is generally referred to as the rigging. These are termed central, triangular and double – each of which could have slightly different variations. If the double is to be used it is most important that these are coupled (i.e. that the two straps have a connecting strap between them). From a saddle fitter's perspective, the rigging is better attached directly to the tree (see photo 67), as skirt-attached rigging can lead to extreme pressure being levied at the edges of the skirt.

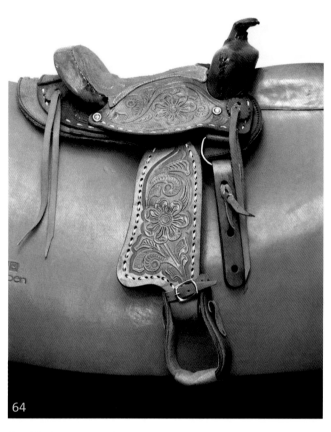

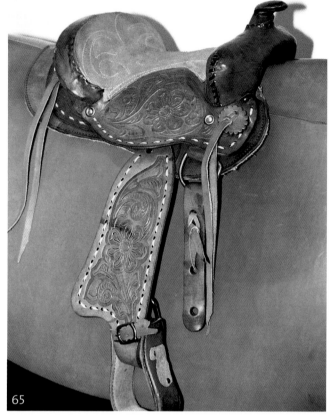

64–66. Three views of a Western saddle, showing the large panel.

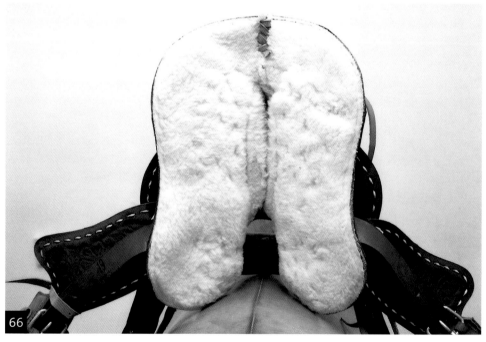

67

The Australian Stock Saddle

As the name implies, the Australian stock saddle originated as a working saddle designed for riding over considerable distances for many hours at a time. In that regard, it has antecedents in common with the Western saddle and, as can be seen from the photos in this section, it is not dissimilar from the Western saddle, although it tends to be smaller and lighter. The two saddles illustrated are both of what is known as the 'swinging fender' design and the girth is attached directly to the tree (see photo 70).

Nowadays, again in common with Western saddles, many stock saddles have fibreglass trees. Photos 68–70 show a saddle with a thin felt panel which has slightly flared skirts to the rear in order not to place undue pressure on the horse's lumbar region. Photo 71 shows a stock saddle with a conventional type of flocked panel. My reservation about this particular design is that, in my view, it is likely to cause discomfort to the horse in the lumbar area; it can, however, be adjusted in much the same way as a flock-filled saddle of conventional design. This particular saddle is marketed as a polocrosse saddle – a sport for which it is regarded as ideal, giving the rider great security because of the very deep seat and the large forward leg swells. (As mentioned in the section on Polo Saddles, stock saddles are also used sometimes for that sport.)

As you can see from photo 72, the saddle shown is characteristically fairly narrow and has a very high pommel. This tree would be most suitable for a

68–70. Three views of an Australian stock saddle with thin panel, flared skirts and girth attachment direct to tree.

high-withered horse (common as a type for herding stock in Australia) and would plainly be unsuitable for a wide-fitting Cob type, with a flat back and low withers.

All the basic saddle fitting points covered in detail in the next chapter would apply to the stock saddle, with the possible exception of the length of panel, which would almost always come further back than would be acceptable in a European saddle. With the felt panel design (photo 73) the flare at the rear of the panel should be sufficient to avoid causing problems. The saddle in photo 71 would need to be fitted with extreme caution, with reference to my earlier remarks about fit in the lumbar region. However, the flocking of this saddle, as shown in photo 74, does allow for careful adjustment.

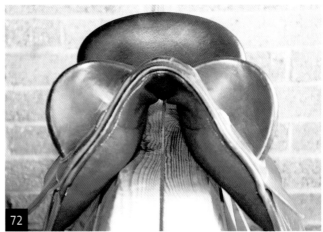

71. Australian stock saddle with conventionally flocked panel.

72. Characteristically narrow stock saddle, with very high pommel.

73. Felt panels should follow the contour of the individual horse's back and should never bridge (see page 67 and photo 113) but, well fitted, they do give very low pressure per square inch on the horse's back.

74. Flocked panels can be adjusted but great care must be taken not to have an area of high pressure under the rear of the saddle beyond the last rib.

Spanish and Portuguese Saddles

As can be seen from photos 75–77, there seem at first sight to be many similarities between the Western saddle and the Spanish and Portuguese designs. But once we get past the large panel and large, comfortable seat, that's really where the similarity ends. As you can see from photo 78, the front profile of the saddle is incredibly severe, with a very narrow gullet. Every saddle of this origin I have seen has been of similar proportions and has often been fitted to a horse with large shoulders and considerable width. In my experience, many horses saddled in this way develop very sore areas indeed behind the shoulders. The reasons for this will become obvious when I detail the correct way to fit a saddle in the next chapter.

Side-saddles

Side-saddle riding has an obvious and fundamental difference from other forms of riding, in that it is the only form in which the rider does not sit astride the horse. However, while this means that some of the 'mechanics' of side-saddle riding are markedly different from riding astride, the underlying principles of equitation continue to apply. Much the same can be said about side-saddles and their fitting: any saddle, for any purpose, has to carry the weight of the rider in a manner that permits the horse to move freely and have as little weight loading per square inch as possible, and the rider has to sit in a position of security, comfort and effectiveness. This being so, the principles of tree angle, panel fit and balance that apply to other saddles apply also to side-saddles. However, because of the fundamental differences in design, and the rider's seat, it is necessary to look at the construction and fitting of side-saddles as a separate issue.

The Tree

As in all treed saddles, the shape of the tree is of fundamental importance in the side-saddle. A major feature is that the nearside tree point is much longer, in order to prevent the saddle from working to the left with the rider on board (see photos 79–81). Note, also, that the trees are built slightly wider on the left towards the rear, to allow for the fact that the belly of the saddle will be built out a little more on that side.

OPPOSITE PAGE
75–78. The Spanish and Portuguese saddles are obviously built for rider comfort, with a deep, luxurious sheepskin-covered seat. The large panel (photo 75) is considered to give the horse's back less pressure, but note the very narrow gullet (photo 76) and the acute angle at the pommel arch (photo 78) which would be far too severe for most horses – even though the saddle shown is regarded as a 'medium' fitting. Other points of interest are the stirrup design (photo 75) and the crupper, usually found on saddles of this type (photo 77).

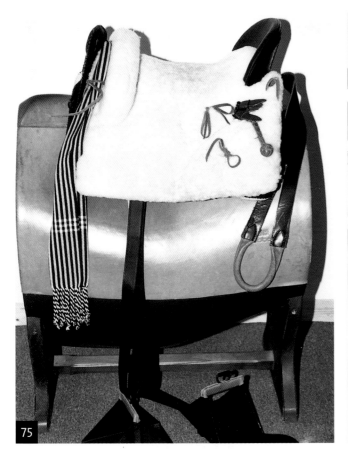

75

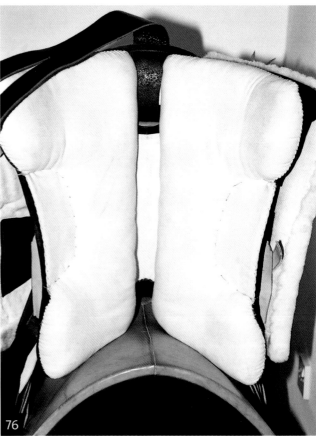

76

77

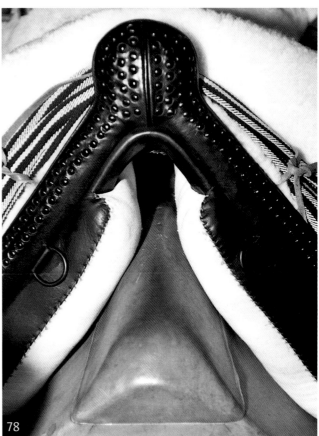

78

79–81. Views of two side-saddle trees. In each photo, the tree on the left is an Aulton and Butler pony tree; that on the right is an older tree for more Thoroughbred types.

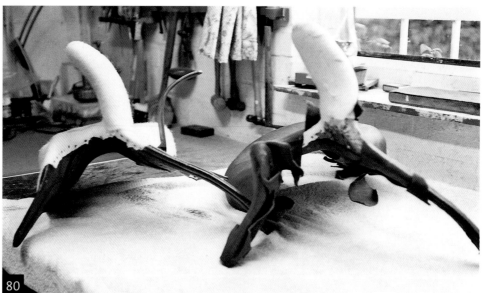

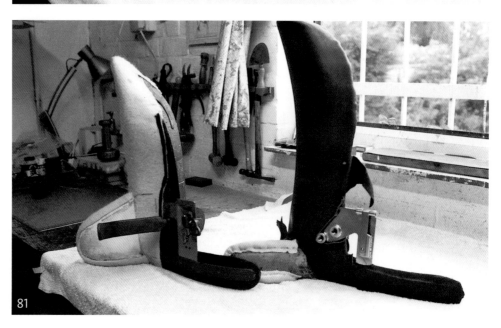

As with many other trees, side-saddle trees were traditionally made of beech-wood, but many new ones are made of synthetic materials, with reinforcements of carbon fibre rather than the traditional steel. These materials produce a much lighter, but very strong framework.

In the photo sequence of the two trees, that on the right in each photo is the older model. Compared to the Aulton and Butler pony tree on the left, it is nar-rower in the arch and points, with the waist area angled slightly to fit more of a Thoroughbred type, whereas the Aulton and Butler is very wide at the front and flat through the waist to accommodate a wider, more rotund shape. The older tree is also reinforced with a half-inch steel bar on the front arch for extra strength. Modern tree-makers say that today's steel is strong enough not to require such additional reinforcement. The older tree has been fitted with a Mayhew quick-release stirrup leather fastening, and the other tree with an Owen design.

The Seat

So far as the seat is concerned, some old side-saddles were made with a waist on the offside. However, in a side-saddle, this does not give any support to the right leg, which is the one that takes the rider's weight, thus the edge of the seat should be shaped to accommodate the leg.

The left belly (panel) is made approximately a quarter of an inch higher than the right one, to give support under the left seat bone; it is also waisted (shaped in) and down into the flap so that the left leg does not rest on a ridge.

Although the seat appears to be flat it is, in fact, shaped (dipped) very slightly to allow for the fact that the rider's thigh is thicker at the top (see photo 82).

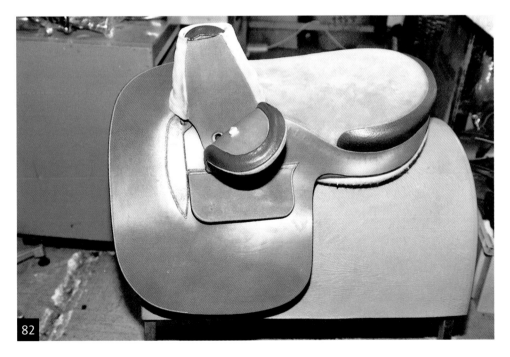

82. Photo showing shape of seat and the fixed and leaping heads. Note, also, the queen on the fixed head.

Fixed and Leaping Heads

On the nearside of the side-saddle are the fixed and leaping heads (upper and lower respectively, see photo 82), around which the rider's legs are positioned. On a side-saddle, these features are also referred to as pommels, although they are obviously different from the pommel of an astride saddle. Flared forms of fixed head are more popular, but choice really depends on the shape of the rider's legs and what fits them. A rider with short, plump legs may find a flared pommel difficult to get their right leg around and it may also push the left hip back; in such cases a straighter (but not necessarily too narrow) pommel would be better. Also, the shape of the rider's leg determines the position of the fixed head. A plumper leg needs the head more to the left (nearside) of the saddle and a thin leg needs the head more upright and to the centre. A 'queen' can be used to fill out the fixed head for a slimmer leg, but a chunky leg will always be uncomfortable in an upright head that pushes the leg to the right. Queen is a fancy name for a sleeve to go over a head – it can be made of anything, from leather to match the saddle through to Gamgee covered in Vetwrap.

Some saddles have dual leaping head fittings. These can be used for jumping (higher, more forward position) or flatwork, or just for a better position for the leg. The nearside flap is extended to the front by a few inches; this keeps the right leg off the horse's shoulder.

Photo 83 shows a Victorian saddle with narrower heads. This design is nowadays less favoured than the more modern designs.

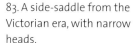
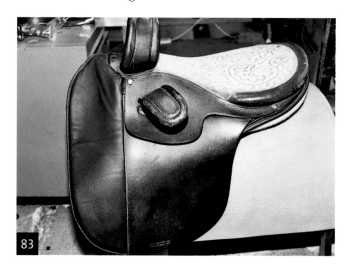

83. A side-saddle from the Victorian era, with narrow heads.

Panel

With side-saddles, as with astride saddles, there should be sufficient clearance through the gullet. The side-saddle is, however, flocked differently from the astride (see photo 84). On the left there is a little more flocking under the long point to encourage the saddle over to the right. This tapers to a very thin section at the top by the scapula. The rear is flocked up higher on the nearside than the offside (about a quarter of an inch, although this can vary). The rear of the offside panel is slightly lower than the nearside, tapering to thinner in the middle, and is quite full at the offside front top. The bottom of the offside is kept quite thin under the short point. Too much flocking at the base here will actually encourage the saddle to go to the left, which is not what is required. Traditionally, panels made of serge are better for the horse's back and easier to adjust.

84. Side-saddle panel.

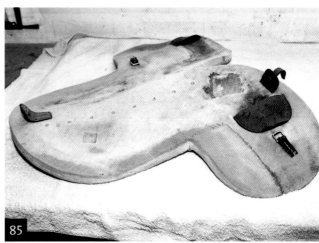

85. A Wykeham pad.

Wykeham pads (see photo 85) are used for closer contact and are good for rounder-shaped horses. They are made of wool felt and are easy to adjust, as wedges are cut to shape and stitched into position on the top of the pad beneath the saddle. They can, in fact, be covered with leather and linen to look like a panel. These pads were traditionally used in circumstances where a rider had one saddle but wished to adapt it quickly to fit several horses, for example when changing horses out hunting. Each horse had his own pad fitted and, since the pads are held on to the saddle by just three buckles, the saddle could be changed quickly, the only constraint being that the horses had to be broadly suited to the same basic size of tree.

Fitting a Side-saddle

Assuming that the tree fits, when the saddle is placed on the horse's back it should initially sit to the right of the horse's spine when viewed from behind (see photo 86). It is also tilted to the right; these factors will correct themselves and the saddle will centralize when the rider is on board. The balance strap is positioned at the widest part of the offside of the saddle and holds the saddle still (see photo 88). The balance girth, which goes from the long point on the front left to the balance strap, should not be over-tightened.

When mounted, the rider's spine should be in line with the horse's spine and the centre of the saddle. Viewed from behind, there is no difference in the upper body from that of an astride rider (see photo 87). Photo 88 shows a side-saddle under load and, in this case, the saddle is sitting out of balance in that it too low behind; it should be absolutely flat (this can be achieved with panel adjustment).

86. View from behind showing that when the side-saddle is placed on the horse's back it should initially sit to the right of the horse's spine. It will centralize with the rider on board, as seen in photo 87.

87. When mounted, the rider's spine should be in line with the horse's spine and the centre of the saddle, which has, itself, centralized.

88. Side-saddle under load – in this case, a little adjustment of the panel is required.

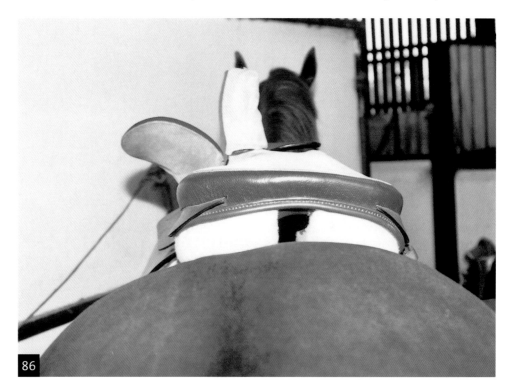

CHAPTER 3

Saddle Fitting

Q UALIFIED SADDLE FITTERS identify a number of specific stages in the process – in fact, in the United Kingdom a Qualified Saddle Fitter will undertake a minimum of sixteen prescribed stages, sometimes more, in order to obtain an excellent fitting for both horse and rider. Broadly, however, the process can be split into the following sections:

1. Gathering background information about the rider, the rider's requirements and the horse's general conformation and condition.

2. A physical check of the horse.

3. Static testing of saddles.

4. Ridden testing and final selection.

5. Post-purchase checks.

Since these processes lie at the core of what saddle fitters and owners are trying to achieve, we will study them, and associated issues, in some detail.

Background Information

The initial contact, often by telephone, requires the saddle fitter to gain a really good mental picture of the horse and rider to be fitted. The information required will include the following points.

For the Horse: size and age of horse, breeding if known, an indication of conformation (high, low or medium withers; long, standard or short back; whether croup-high; general condition and state of fitness) and whether there is, or have been, any back problems, unlevelness or physical asymmetry.

For the Rider: rider's height, weight, age, length of leg between hip and knee and discipline for which the saddle is required.

In respect of the intended usage, any preferences on the rider's part regarding a deep or flat seat, size of knee rolls, style of flap, colour or manufacturer should also be noted – although the horse's conformation may, in some cases, have an influence on the precise details of design. Once these details are to hand, the saddle fitter should be able to select a range of saddles likely to suit requirements.

Assessing Conformation

In respect of the background information on the horse mentioned above, it will be useful at this point to examine the influence that conformation and action can have on selecting the best saddle for a particular horse. Obviously, Qualified Saddle Fitters will apply their expertise when confronted with a horse in the flesh, but a general appreciation of how important these factors can be may help horse owners to provide as much information as possible in advance of the visit. This will help the saddle fitter to establish a fairly realistic picture, so that a broadly suitable range of saddles can be selected.

It is true to say that the characteristics of many breeds are fairly consistent. For example, an English Thoroughbred will usually be of slim, athletic build and have medium to high or very high withers. Although there are many types of Cob, most will be strong, stocky, and usually flat-backed, with large shoulders and low or visually non-existent withers. In addition to the Welsh and Irish Cobs, other breeds that will have a similar shape to what is generally regarded as a Cob profile will be the Dales and Highland. Also some Quarter Horses and Morgans fall into this category. The Arab, however, comes in so many shapes and sizes as to almost defy generalization. For example, the 'English' Arab will be small, short-backed and often flat along the spine, with very little in respect of withers and large shoulders. However, the Egyptian Arab will be taller and rather more like a slightly scaled down English Thoroughbred, while Eastern European Arabs can be almost any shape and size. With no disrespect to the breed, when the word 'Arab' is used to describe a horse to be fitted, the saddler fitter knows there is work to be done, for they are very rarely straightforward.

A medium fit saddle is what most saddle fitters would hope and expect to work with most of the time, since this relates to a horse whose conformation would generally regarded to be the norm – that is, a healthy standard back, neither croup-high, dipped, nor roached, symmetrical shoulders, not particularly high or low at the withers, and level, straight movement. However, patently not all horses are 'medium' and it will be useful to assess a few 'types' with a saddle fitter's eye.

Ageing Thoroughbred: Photo 89 shows Charlie, an English Thoroughbred, twenty-three years old, 17 hands, healthy and sound. However, in common with most Thoroughbreds of his age and stature, he is what I would describe as rangy; his top line and musculature have fallen away and he has steeple withers. He will, in all probability, continue to be a good ride for some time; however, he is fairly difficult to fit. Because he has fallen away substantially just behind the shoulders and his back has a number of fairly prominent vertebrae he would require very accurate and experienced fitting. He may well need a saddle tree shaped as in photo 90; he will also need a wide gullet as well as a tree head that will permit the scapulae to rotate accurately and fully; he will almost certainly need a tree with

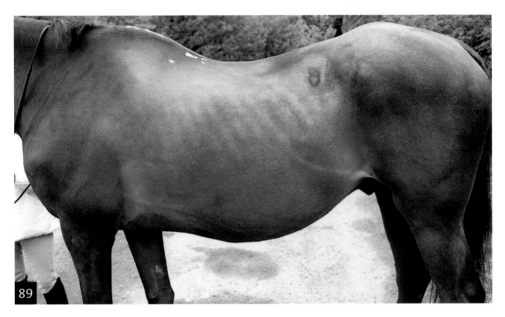

89 and 90. Photo 89 shows Charlie, an aged Thoroughbred (see text). Although he is sound and healthy, horses of his age and type can be difficult to fit and he will require as saddle such as that shown in photo 90.

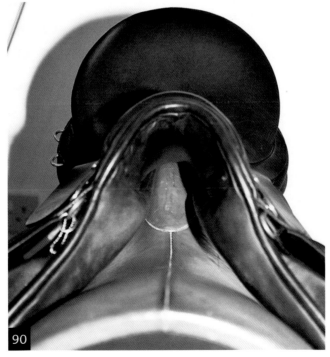

a substantially cut back head to avoid any possibility of contact with the top of the withers.

Some 'alternative' system saddle fitting practitioners will claim that a horse of this type should have a very wide fitting tree, supported by many saddle blankets or padding of one sort of another to permit the top line to improve with work. While I try very hard to keep my mind open to new ideas, I have never once seen a horse of this age and type benefit from an over-wide saddle but I have, however, seen many badly damaged withers when this alternative system of fitting has been adopted.

Cob: Photo 91 shows Hector, a five-year-old Cob, standing 14.2 hands. Hector's breeding is uncertain – his owner feels he may be Highland x Section D – but he has a very normal sort of Cob conformation and shares aspects of this with many of the large native breeds. He has a back which many people would describe as a table top, with virtually no withers and substantial shoulders (see photo 92). Animals of this type are notoriously difficult to fit, as they tend to throw saddles off to one side or the other and saddles frequently slip forward in downward transitions. Hector is what would generally be regarded as an extra wide or even an extra, extra wide tree fitting. This back profile will often benefit from a fairly shallow seat, and will almost always require a point and balance strap as shown in photo 93.

Photos 91 and 92 show Hector's typical Cob conformation (see text). He will require a saddle with point and balance straps, as shown in photo 93.

91

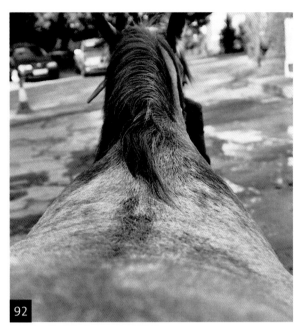

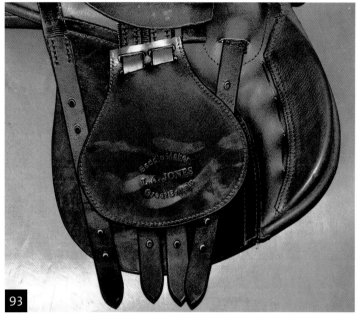

Arab: As mentioned earlier, one hesitates to say that Arabs have a normal shape. Apart from the variations deriving from different breed lines, they can be almost anything from 14 hands to 16 hands or more high. Photos 94–96 show something of the variety. Saddle fittings may range from extra, extra wide for those with short, dipped backs to medium/narrow for those with long, straight backs. However, what is beyond question is that the Arab, whatever its breed line and type, requires very considerable expertise in fitting.

The Dipped Back: Photo 97 shows a particularly extreme example of a dipped back. This horse is twelve years old, but the owner assures me that he has had this conformation defect for his entire life. Despite this, he is a Medium level dressage horse – and yes, we did manage to fit a saddle. This was, however, one of those rare occasions (see The Delights and Drawbacks of a Bespoke Saddle in Chapter 3) when a saddle had to be made especially for this horse, on what is usually termed a 'banana' tree with a panel specially designed and fitted (requiring three visits).

The Asymmetrical Horse: Photo 98 shows the considerable difference between the shoulders of this particular horse, indeed it is like looking down the spine of two different horses stuck together. Nevertheless, this photo was taken when the animal was standing completely square on a flat, level surface. This kind of problem is very prevalent in many Cobs and native breeds and will almost always mean that saddles will be thrown substantially to one side. A horse who has very uneven hip movement will have the same effect. Asymmetry and the ways of overcoming these problems are discussed in more detail later – see Saddle Moving to One Side in Chapter 4.

94

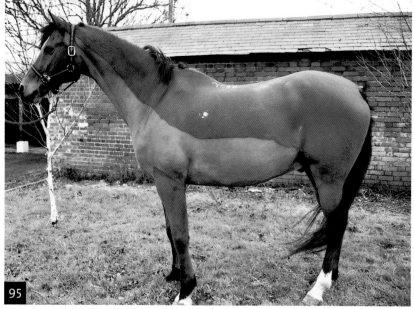

94–96. Three photos to show something of the variety among Arabs. Charlemagne (photo 94) is 14.2 hands; to many eyes he might look like a 'typical' Arab: Danny Boy (photo 95) is a Polish Russian standing 16.2 hands: Nowat (photo 96) is also Polish Russian, but a hand smaller at 15.2 hands.

95

96

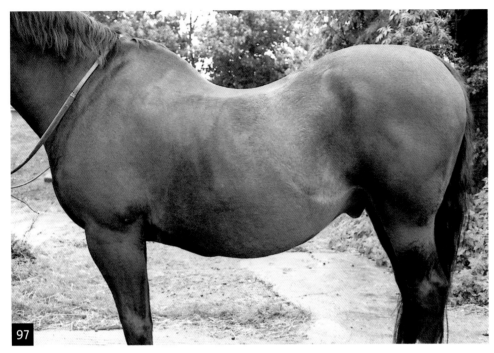

97. A major fitting problem posed by a severely dipped back. This was one of the rare occasions on which it was necessary to provide a bespoke saddle with a 'banana' tree. Note, also, the problematical girth groove position.

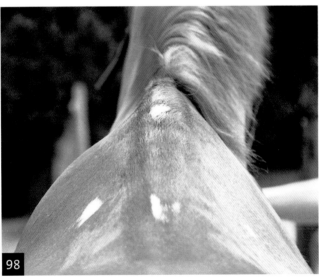

98. Asymmetrical horse: the nearside shoulder is much larger than the offside: note also the white pressure marks.

The Croup-high Horse: The horse who is croup-high will always tend to throw saddles forward, as his movement does, in effect, throw the rider forward ('down-hill'). The solution to this problem is discussed in Chapter 4.

Extravagant Action: When one thinks of unusual and extravagant gaits these can be best characterized by breeds such as the Hackney, or horses used for pacing, and some of the breeds with breed-specific gaits which appear in American show classes. Obviously, fitting saddles to horses with such action requires even more expertise than fitting those with gaits regarded as normal, as these extraordinary

99. A croup-high horse, whose movement will tend to throw the saddle forwards.

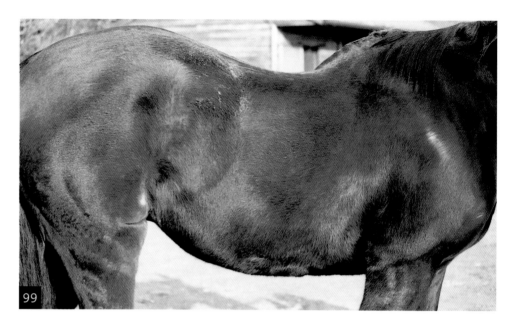

forms of movement are often related to unusual conformation. In some cases, saddle manufacturers do take account of the movement of particular breeds. For example, the Icelandic pony has a fast, four-beat gait called the tölt and some saddles are made specifically for riding this breed in this gait. Similarly, Lane Fox show saddles accommodate the movements of some of the American breeds. Hackneys, however, were bred primarily for driving and I am not aware of any manufacturer producing a saddle for this particular breed, even though one frequently sees full- and part-bred Hackneys ridden under saddle.

The Physical Check

With as much information to hand as possible, and a selection of saddles chosen on that basis, the saddle fitter now attends the premises where the horse is kept, to meet the client, along with the client's instructor and groom (as appropriate) and, of course, the horse.

I should say at this juncture that, while it may be relevant, even helpful, to have a professional instructor and/or groom present at the saddle fitting, they should be there for the entire procedure, including the back examination, the several eliminations and the dynamic tests, which we will discuss in due course. It is simply not acceptable for someone to waltz in at the end of the saddle fitting and say 'I don't like this saddle', 'I don't like this model' or 'I don't like the way it fits'. Fortunately, such discourteous behaviour is rare and, where it occurs, is more the province of the inexperienced and part-qualified than of the genuinely knowledgeable. However, this brings me to the next point. While a genuine friend – perhaps someone who helps with the horse – may be welcome at the fitting if they keep their counsel, the self-styled 'friend' is not. This is the person – often the yard

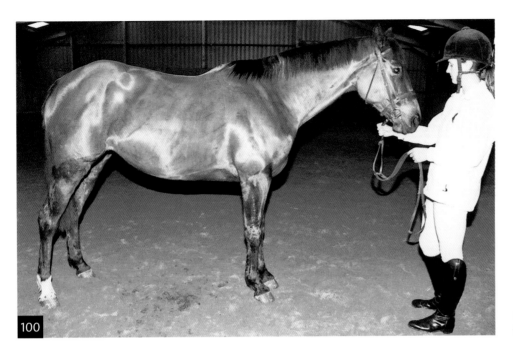

100

100. A horse nicely presented for the saddle fitting.

'know-it-all' – who is almost always unqualified and yet full of 'good' (normally totally inappropriate) advice, who will endeavour to tell the Qualified Saddle Fitter how to fit saddles. This is not only rude and disrespectful, but also rather foolish. It is to be hoped that such a person will be pulling ragwort at the crucial time.

More constructively (and more likely), it is to be hoped that the horse to be fitted will be dry, clean and bridled (a headcollar is acceptable but a bridle gives rather more control). The vast majority of clients do present their horses nicely turned out – as in photo 100 – which is a relief because saddle fitters really don't want new saddles to become unnecessarily marked. There is also another very important reason for ensuring that the horse is well groomed before a new saddle is fitted. As part of the fitting process, the rider will try out all the saddles that have been short-listed by the saddle fitter. When each saddle is removed it will leave an outline on the well-groomed horse's back. Every picture tells a story and the saddle fitter will like to see a clear, unbroken line that is not blurred or fuzzy. This assists in checking that the bearing surfaces are correct and that the saddle is not moving excessively.

I do, however, recall a case in which the horse to be fitted was turned out in an extremely muddy paddock. He was plastered; presumably one of those rare animals who enjoy a mud bath on the basis of 'there's nothing quite like it for cooling the blood'. This mud was that nasty, sticky, yellowish-grey type which made it impossible to identify the colour of his coat, and his mane and tail were equally caked. The owner was nowhere in sight! I inquired about her whereabouts and was told, casually, that she was always a very bad time-keeper and no, she couldn't be contacted because she didn't have a mobile telephone. Fortunately, I had arranged to fit saddles for two horses stabled only a mile or two away and I left saying that I would be returning about three hours later, by which time I expected the horse to have been brought in, bathed and dried off.

When I got back to the yard, I found the horse unrecognizable in his clean and dry state, with the owner very apologetic. The horse was actually a nice Riding Club type, well muscled and in good condition. He was very pleasant to handle and easy to fit, which was some consolation after the earlier delay. I did consider charging the owner for my wasted time, but finally relented! Fortunately, this sort of situation is a rarity.

Assuming that the horse is correctly presented, the saddle fitter should first seek to establish a friendship with him and inquire about any behavioural problems, such as kicking out, biting and resistance to girthing. In addition to preserving self and valuable tack, such inquiries may also provide information relevant to the process of saddle fitting – for example, attempting to bite or resisting being girthed may suggest prior or ongoing pain associated with being saddled.

Even if the horse appears perfectly calm and comfortable, the next step is for the saddle fitter to conduct a thorough back examination. The horse should be stood on flat, hard ground, standing square with weight on all four legs. Initially, the examination will entail running the tips of the fingers along the spine, looking for any sign discomfort or soreness. The overall condition of the back will be noted and commented on. Checks should be carried out on both the back and the girth groove of any bald patches, scars, lumps and bumps (both hard and soft). Specific checks are then made on the musculature. On each side of the horse, the trapezius area behind each scapula is checked with the saddle fitter's fingertips, applying firm pressure, running from the trapezius area, approximately two inches away from the spine, up to the lumbar area along the latissimus and longissimus dorsi. At this point, for reasons I will explain shortly, the sacroiliac area is also checked. The next step is to check the symmetry of the back and the symmetry and evenness of the shoulders. The view for this check is taken from directly behind, close in, looking down the spine. It is essential at this point that the horse is standing square, in order that any asymmetry in the shoulders can be properly observed and noted. With animals of any size, it will be necessary for the saddle fitter to stand on a box or something similar to make this check efficiently, and it is at this point that prior knowledge of any tendency for the horse to kick may prove invaluable.

Assuming all is well, a flex test is then performed, to each side in turn, with the horse standing so that the flex is taken around the slightly leading foreleg. The horse is encouraged to undertake this flexing by use of a carrot or other titbit and it is anticipated that he will be able to bring his muzzle as far as the girth area. If the horse is not able to bend through the neck but consistently moves around the

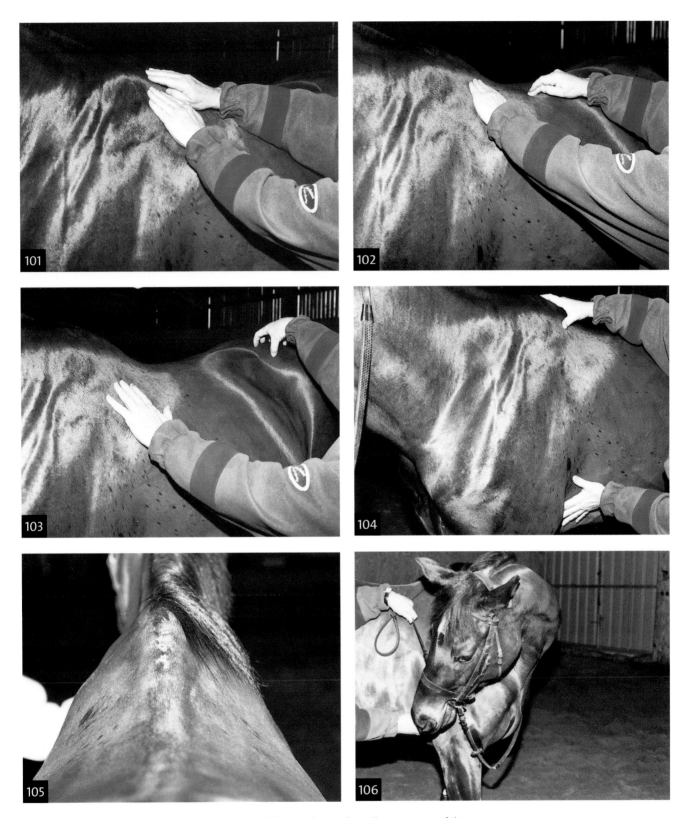

101–106. These photos show the sequence of the
back examination and the flex test.

foreleg and swings the quarters to reach the carrot, this lack of flexion is noted. After this test, the fitter may well take a template of the horse's back to retain as a record. (This template is often taken at a later stage, towards the end of the fitting.) If all is satisfactory, the horse will then be walked and trotted for the fitter to establish evenness of hip lift and soundness (see photo 107).

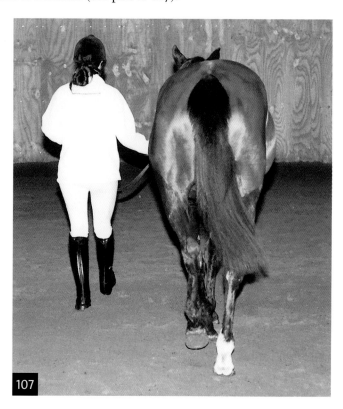

107. Checking for evenness of movement.

The Need to Understand the Horse's Movement

Further to the physical checks just detailed, I should stress that an understanding of the way the horse moves is essential not only for professional saddle fitters, but for anyone who wants to increase their general knowledge of saddle fitting.

The horse's hindquarters are his powerhouse: the energy generated by the hindquarters passes through the back to the forehand, providing the basis for forward movement. If, for any reason, a horse is unable to 'work through' from behind, he is compelled to 'pull' himself along from the front end.

If, for example, through a slip or a fall, the ligamentous attachments holding the sacroiliac joint together become stretched or misaligned (or, indeed, there is damage to another hind limb joint), the horse loses the ability to get the hind leg far enough under his body on the affected side. A horse with this type of problem will rarely appear 'lame' but will go 'short' in the relative hind leg. The problem is exacerbated – and will become most noticeable – when the affected limb is the outside leg when the horse is asked to canter.

Invariably there will be muscle spasm in the gluteus medius muscle (the large muscle over the sacroiliac joint). Loss of movement of the sacroiliac joint invariably results in stiffness in the back, giving the horse a rigid appearance. A horse who has had this problem for a long time will display shortening of the hamstrings, tightness in the biceps femoris and semitendinous muscles and the latissimus dorsi muscle will also be affected.

The easiest way to identify a problem in the sacroiliac region is to apply light pressure to the gluteus medius muscle. This is done by lining up over the point of the hip and pressing on the top of the rump. A sound horse should not dip away, so any significant dipping should be referred to a veterinary practitioner.

If any significant tenderness, soreness, or lack of flexibility is apparent during the physical checks, the saddle fitter will have to decide whether it is wise to carry on with the saddle fitting at that time or advise the client to consult their veterinary surgeon or a qualified back practitioner. Although saddle fitters may well have the knowledge and skill to detect problems with backs and gait malfunctions, it is not part of their remit to give specific advice in these areas, much less to offer treatment.

If, however, there are just minor areas of discomfort, and particularly if it is obvious to the saddle fitter that these are the direct result of a badly fitting saddle which is about to be remedied, the process can continue.

Happily, most horses presented for fittings do not have major problems and one can proceed straight away.

The Static Tests

The saddles will now be placed directly onto the horse's back without a numnah, blanket or any other sort of covering and each saddle subjected to a seven-point check. The fitter will explain this sequence and its aims to the client. Only those saddles passing all points of this check will be put onto a short list. Although the figures may vary from client to client, and horse to horse, on average a short list of four or five satisfactory saddles from perhaps a dozen or so tried will be the order of the day.

The Seven Points of Saddle Fitting

The seven prescribed points to check are as follows. (These are the most significant of the sixteen points referred to at the start of this chapter.)

1. The front of the tree and the points have to be at a similar angle to the trapezius area upon which they will rest. The tolerance level is certainly no more than 10 degrees (see photo 108). At this point, care must be taken to ensure that the angle is that of the tree and not of the facing at the front of the panel, as these two angles do not necessarily coincide.

108. Checking the angulation of the tree and the trapezius area.

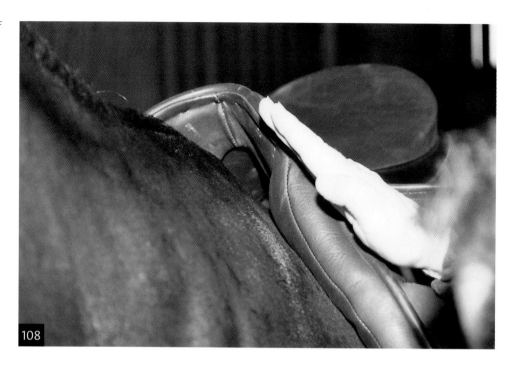

As one can see quite readily, if the saddle is too wide a fitting, there are two major problems for the horse and one major problem for the rider. First, the underside of the arch may well be in contact with the horse's withers. Additionally, there may be too much pressure exerted at the base of the arch on each side of the gullet. This, of course, will depend upon the horse's conformation – some Thoroughbred types are very narrow throughout the whole trapezius area but an aged Cob for example, may broaden rapidly at the base of the withers. In any event, the saddle will sit too low in the front, which will throw the rider's weight forward, causing pressure on the front of the saddle to be increased drastically and throwing the rider off the seat bones onto the fork.

If the saddle is too narrow, the probability is that the area directly underneath the points of the tree will be subject to extreme pressure in this very small region and the saddle will appear to be sitting uphill, with the rider's weight being thrown back onto the buttocks and the horse's lumbar area. Saddles with this fitting fault will often also bridge (see photo 113). It is not always possible to get good sight of the tree itself as, on some saddles, the tree is inside the panel – but a competent saddle fitter will know how best to judge this.

2. With the saddle off load, that is without a rider on and without being girthed up, one should be able to slide one hand evenly and easily the length of the tree from the gullet to the point without undue pressure (see photo 114). If this pressure is uneven or has any 'hot spots' this will probably indicate that the tree itself is either too wide or too narrow. *Note that this is an off-load test.* It is absolutely not correct to do as many riders do – trying to slip a hand between the horse's trapezius area and the front of the saddle when the horse

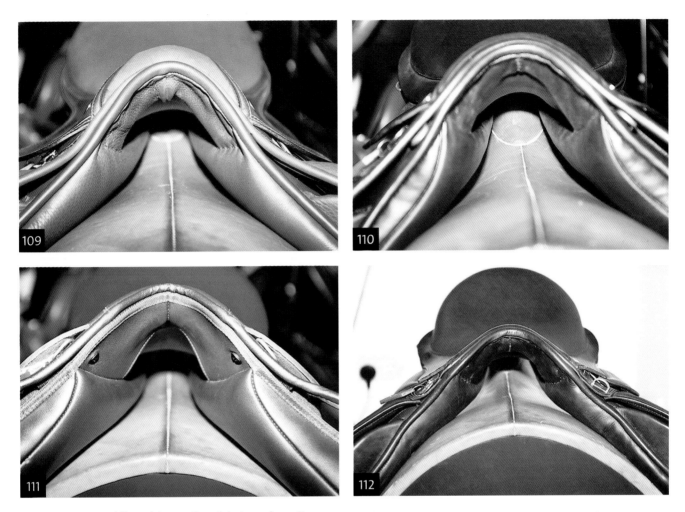

109–112. Various saddle widths: medium (photo 109); medium-wide (110); wide (111) and extra wide (112).

113. A saddle bridging badly on a Cob – note space beneath the saddle.

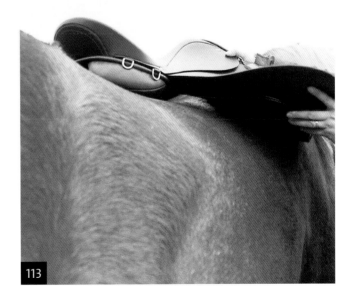

is girthed up and the rider is on board and then declare it too tight. What we are testing for is an uneven angle, and this can only be discerned properly with the saddle off load.

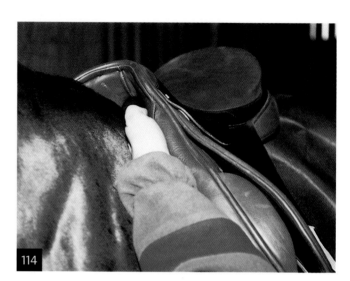

114. With the saddle off load and not girthed up, one should be able to slide one hand evenly and easily the length of the tree from the gullet to the point.

below Diagram to show correct and incorrect width fittings.

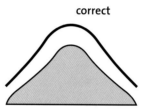

correct

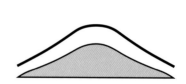

tree angle, front elevation

incorrect

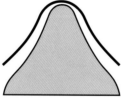

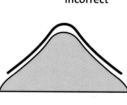

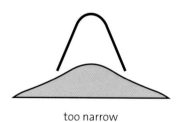

too wide   too narrow

3. The next point is to ensure that the gullet is wide enough not to impinge on either side of the spine (see photos 115 and 116). This is particularly important with horses with high withers, for example, aged Thoroughbreds. However, this is where saddle design and fitting are very specific – while 'wide enough' is very important, 'too wide' creates a new set of problems. At the one extreme, with a narrow gullet, the edges of the gullet may clamp tightly each side of the vertebrae, causing extreme discomfort and trauma. However, a gullet which is far too wide must inevitably reduce the sides of the panel – that is to say, there is a far smaller area to support the weight of the rider and, the greater the

loading per square inch, the more chance there is of bruising. Thus there is a median to be found: a gullet wide enough so that the spinal processes are not contacted directly, but not so wide as to significantly reduce the weight-bearing area. Further to this, the gullet must be of an adequate width along its entire length and not just across the front – this is of particular importance to those horses with a fairly prominent spine throughout the whole of the saddle region.

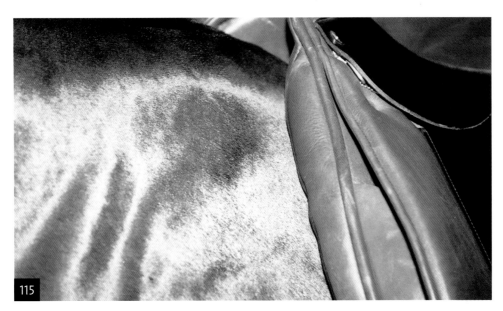

115 and 116. The gullet must be sufficiently wide not to impinge on either side of the spine.

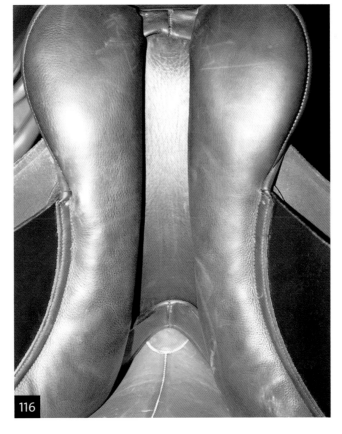

4. This is the test which everyone 'knows' and almost everyone gets wrong – how many fingers should fit between the top of the withers and the underside of the saddle arch? Some riding organizations will tell you a minimum of three fingers (see photo 117). This is total tosh! The answer is that there should be sufficient clearance under load under all circumstances. It may well be three fingers. On close-contact saddles, it may be one and a half. Plainly, on a very deep-seated saddle, there is likely to be rather more clearance than with a flat saddle, so one cannot be pedantic. In any event whose fingers are we talking about – a large man with fat fingers or a small girl with slim fingers?

117. The 'minimum of three fingers' test (here, four) which, in many circumstances, is misleading and incorrect. This photo does, however, show a saddle sitting in good balance.

With reference to a small girl's fingers, and to illustrate my point further, I might add that I was once asked to check a saddle that had been fitted by an eleven-year-old girl. I'm serious! The mother told me, quite firmly, that her daughter was a member of the local Pony Club and therefore 'knows about these things' and that she was sure it was 'perfect'! Fortunately, the second-hand saddle was on approval. Asked to explain her saddle fitting procedure and how she had applied her knowledge of saddle fitting, the little girl proudly inserted three of her fingers under the arch of the saddle. That was it! This particular saddle sat up in front but produced pressure points elsewhere on the pony's back.

I felt sorry for the little girl, who had only been putting into practice what she had been told. I explained that 'three fingers' had absolutely nothing to do with checking the fit of a saddle, that 'adequate clearance throughout the entire gullet' was the measure and that much depends on the saddle type and design. For example, being able to insert three fingers under the arch of a close-contact saddle would mean that it didn't fit!

I was later contacted by the DC of the Pony Club to which the little girl belongs – could I please give a talk on saddle fitting?

So, I will repeat that the requirement is *sufficient clearance under all circumstances*. Also, the initial test will be done without the rider's weight, but then checked again after the rider has ridden on the saddle for a few minutes, as some saddle flocking can compress very quickly and some synthetic trees are designed to widen after only a few minutes riding. So this clearance test is more properly carried out at the end of the testing period under load and occasionally can disqualify what was previously thought to be a good candidate for the short list.

5. It is essential the saddle should sit in balance. This *generally* means that the cantle will sit slightly higher than the pommel, as in photo 117; photos 118–120 show deficiencies in this department. 'In balance' signifies that the rider can sit in the centre of the saddle, with weight divided evenly throughout the length of the panel. This particular test requires a really experienced eye as some very deep-seated saddles require the cantle to be a lot higher than the pommel to be in correct balance. This is most often apparent on dressage saddles as so many jumping saddles nowadays have medium to flat seats.

6. The panel should fit evenly all the way through its length and breadth. If the panel is a correct fit it will utilize all of its area – as mentioned previously, the larger the area in contact with the horse, the less pounds per square inch of rider's weight will be transmitted to the horse's back. This should never exceed one and a half pounds per square inch at any point. This is where the type of panel is crucial. For example, a well-filled panel will rapidly mould to the horse's individual contours, therefore maximizing the bearing surface, whereas a close-contact saddle with a moulded panel will need to fit much more precisely as, in some instances, the fillings are hard and unyielding. It is essential, therefore, that close-contact saddles should have a panel fit that mirrors the horse's back – it should not be assumed that they will change shape with work and condition. Photo 121 shows a critical assessment of these factors.

7. The length of panel should not extend beyond the horse's eighteenth rib. Note that this does not extend vertically and therefore this measurement must be gauged directly underneath the rear of the panel (see photo 122). This is an area which often gives problems, particularly when the horse has a short or dipped back and the rider is technically too large for the animal. If a rider is too large or heavy for a particular horse, there may be a temptation to fit a saddle slightly

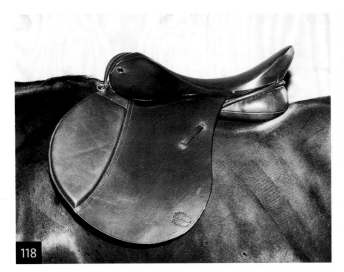

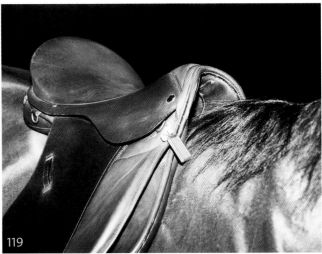

118–120. Deficiencies in balance. In photo 118, the pommel is too high and the tree too narrow; the saddle sits 'uphill'. Photo 119 is another view of too narrow a saddle. The saddle in photo 120 is too wide and sits too low in front; it rocks readily, flipping the cantle (which is far too high) up and down. (The saddle marking from a previous test is clearly visible beneath the rear of the seat.)

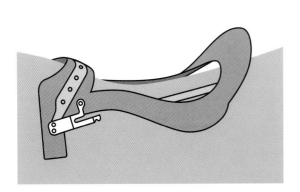

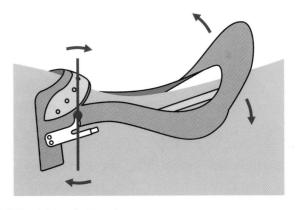

Diagram to show correct fitting of tree (left) and movement of tree caused by incorrect fitting (right).

long in the hope of reducing the panel pressure. However, if this is not done with extreme care, bruising of the lumbar area is almost certain. (In the section on Western Saddles in Chapter 2, we noted differences between Western and English saddles in this respect.)

Hopefully, having carried out these tests, the saddle fitter will have a short list of saddles which will pass on all seven points (see photo 123). The next step is to proceed to the dynamic part of the saddle fitting.

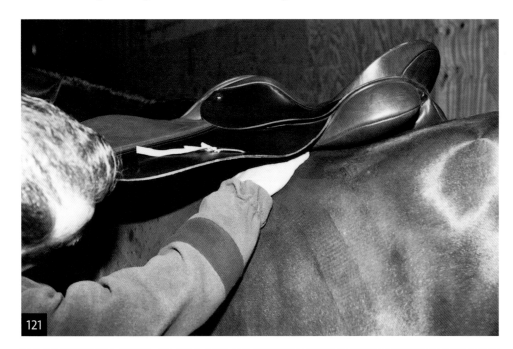

121. The fitting of this saddle, although adequate under the rear gussets, is less than perfect off load.

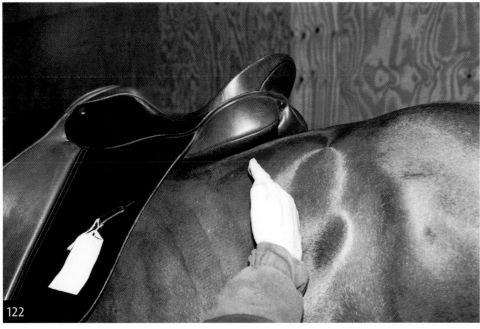

122. Photo to show location and angle of the last rib.

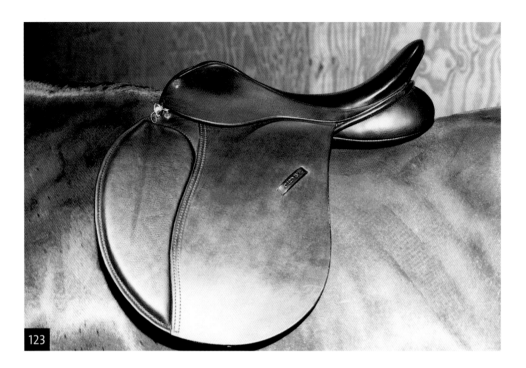

123

The Ridden Test

This is the section within which there can be simply no compromises whatsoever. It is a sad fact of life that saddles which have a very high quality of static fit may fail miserably when ridden in, and such saddles should be disqualified immediately, no matter how much the saddle fitter and client may have favoured them previously.

After the saddle is girthed up, but before the rider mounts, the horse should be walked and trotted away from and then past the saddle fitter (photo 124) as, in this unloaded condition, any movements of the saddle will be magnified. For example, a horse with one shoulder larger than the other will almost always throw the saddle away from the larger shoulder. This is why, on the second part of the static saddle fitting, any saddle should be fitted to the enlarged shoulder, as this will be the seat of any movement. Also, from the side elevation, if the girthing arrangements don't suit the conformation of this particular horse, the saddle is liable to bounce up and down in the area of the rear panel, and wave like a flag from behind.

If this preliminary test proves satisfactory, the rider will mount from a mounting block (not from the ground) adjust the stirrup leathers and girth and proceed to a suitable riding area. This will hopefully be a manège or arena, or at least a flat paddock or field which is not rock hard or soft and slippery. The rider will then be asked to ride the horse in as normal, which must include walk, trot and canter on both reins. At rising trot (see photo 125), particular emphasis will be placed on

124. Saddle still fitting well in trot in hand.

how little the saddle moves under the rear panel (any bouncing up and down being checked from the side and any lateral movement from the rear). When the horse is ridden in satisfactorily, the rider will be asked to do a small circle (10–15 m diameter) in trot on each rein. At some point, the rider should come off the circle (when plainly the saddle will be sitting slightly to the outside of the circle) then go onto a straight line and, within five or six strides, the saddle should centralize (see photos 126 and 127). This exercise should be done on both reins. If the horse is symmetrical, the saddle is symmetrical and the rider sits straight and does not collapse at the hip, the saddle *will* centralize. But of course, in the real world, horses, saddles, and riders are rarely symmetrical and it is highly likely that the saddle will sit more or less to one side of the spine. Therefore, this assessment is best left to the experienced fitter – positively not to the riding instructor. This is not a reflection the riding instructor's qualifications and competence in that role, but they are highly unlikely to be a Qualified Saddle Fitter, and will not be aware of what adjustments can be made to minimize or alleviate such a problem.

Because the horse cannot give a verbal opinion of the saddle, we have to surmise from his reactions whether or not he is happy with the fit and design. The two best exercises to demonstrate this is are lengthened trot and the canter-trot transition. Therefore, the rider will be asked to do a lengthened trot: if the horse does it with ease, it is evident that there is no restriction on forward going and activity. The next step is to ask for an active canter and a good forward transition to trot. On the point of the transition we would hope to see a full extension of the forearm and even a pointing of the toe (see photo 12, page 11). If the horse tends not to want to go forward into trot, but stumbles, or tends to resist and shorten,

125. Checking the saddle in rising trot.

126 and 127. As the rider comes off the circle in trot (photo 126), the saddle is sitting to the right (outside) because of the left bend. Five strides later, on a straight line, the saddle has centralized (photo 127).

this may well be an indication that the saddle is too tight at the front. (This is a test in which some of the saddles with synthetic trees, without metal support, do particularly well).

If the saddle being tried is a general purpose or jumping design, and it is the intention to jump this horse, then plainly one will want to see the horse over a fence or two to ensure that he moves freely and the rider is comfortable and secure over the fence.

If all these tests are completed satisfactorily, the saddle concerned goes forward towards the ultimate choice. This procedure is adopted on all of the short-listed saddles and if any are found defective, or obviously less good than another, they should be rejected, regardless of price, cosmetics and other peripheral criteria. In my experience, by this process of elimination, the best candidate will usually select itself to the satisfaction of the saddle fitter, client and instructor. Just occasionally, however, things do not go quite according to plan, and a degree of re-thinking may be necessary.

Hiccups and Hitches

So far, we have run through a scenario which ends with a saddle that fits the horse correctly, allowing him to move freely throughout a range of exercises, with the rider sitting in a comfortable and secure manner. Everyone is happy. Well, this is where the first problem may occur, perhaps surfacing despite logic, statistical fact and technically correct fit. There are occasions (and many of us riders are well aware of this) when, for whatever reason, a particular horse doesn't seem to go as well as he should or could. The most careful and experienced practitioners in all branches of the horse world are aware that, despite their best efforts, Sod's Law may sometimes take over and spoil the party. In terms of saddle fitting, it sometimes happens that, despite there being no concrete, discernible reason, it is a fact that a horse is not going so well in a selected saddle as he did in another saddle – which either the rider liked less or which, technically, did not seem to be as perfect a fit (or both!). Under such circumstances I have found from long, long experience that the answer is to change the saddle. Yes, you can adjust this and that, make small changes here and there but, at the end of the day, satisfaction can only be achieved when the horse and rider are able to perform their tasks well and efficiently.

Having admitted that this situation *can* arise out of the blue, I have to say that, more often, something similar has occurred after a client has specified that they want a particular designer label or manufacturer, or a model which they have seen on a friend's horse or in a catalogue, and has not been prepared to keep an open mind in respect of other makes or models which may have had a more satisfactory outcome. I always feel uneasy when having a first contact with a client who states categorically that they want this make, this model, this size, this fitting because this is what their friend has and they like it. My first question is, 'Have you tried this particular model on this horse?' The answer is almost always, 'No, but my friend's horse is the same shape and size.' Under these circumstances, I keep an open mind and bring out a large selection of saddles from many makers, based on the description of the horse, the client's physical size and the discipline the saddle is to be used for. I do, of course, also take the type of saddle they have specified but, more often than not, this turns out to be less suitable than other alternatives. However, the customer is king, they pay the piper and (particularly if the saddle they specified is the latest hot fashion item), and no matter how good the advice given, the saddle fitter's opinion may be overruled. But it is the fitter who will be blamed later, if the horse is not going as well as he should.

The Saddle Fitting Certificate and Post-purchase Check

Once a selection has been made, the saddle fitter will complete the saddle fitting certificate (see pages 80–81). This process will include the taking of profiles (see photos 128–131), a weight tape measurement, the noting of any areas of discomfort, old scarring, white marks, etc. and a comment on the general state of the horse's back; a full and accurate description of the horse, a note of the rider's height, weight and age (if appropriate – a child or young adolescent will change size rapidly) and (in the case of the horse having more than one rider) the tallest/heaviest rider. There will also be comments on the fit of the saddle and on the panel mark (see photo 132, page 82) left on the horse after being ridden (which

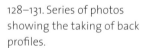

128–131. Series of photos showing the taking of back profiles.

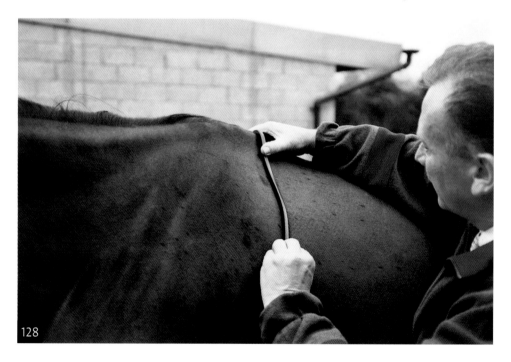

128

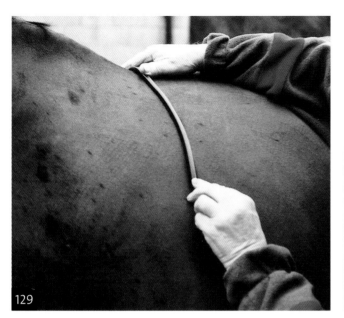

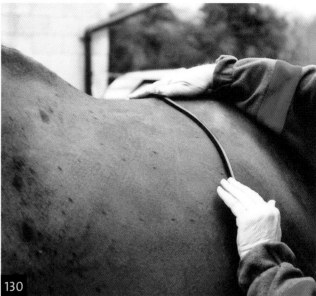

is a good indication of lie and fit) and whether or not a numnah or saddle cloth is to be used. (If this is the case, the selected saddle should be tried with the saddle cloth or numnah on to ensure that it does not adversely affect the fit. However, I would reiterate that, when fitting, it is always advantageous to try the saddles without any type of back covering, which may disguise the analysis of the initial fit.) The information recorded gives guidance to the horse's owner about the frequency of subsequent saddle fitting checks. Furthermore, in the case of a dispute arising, it is available to protect the interests of both horse owner and saddle fitter.

Sample saddle fitting certificate.

SADDLEWORLD
Bart J. Snowball Ltd
www.saddleworld.co.uk email: ken@saddleworld.co.uk
Head office Tel/Fax: 01622 844440 Eve: 01795 522832
Ken mobile: 079895 73281

Client's Name/Address _____

_____

_____ Postcode _____

Tel no. Home _____ Work/Mobile _____

Name of regular rider if different from above _____

Approx. Height/Weight of rider at time of purchase _____ ft _____ in _____ st

Name of Horse/Pony _____ Age _____ Height _____

Breed/Type Colour _____

Distinguishing Marks _____

Any Injuries/Blemishes/Unlevelness at time of fitting _____

_____

Any work being undertaken at present? _____

Work anticipated _____

Details of part exchange _____ £ _____

Other items sold _____ £ _____

Date of saddle purchase _____ £ _____

Credit card handling charge 2.5%   Total £ _____

NEW/SECONDHAND

Brand name _____ Type _____

Width fit _____ Size _____ Ref no. _____

Profile taken YES/NO Please turn over for profile details

Certificate of saddle fitting – Bart J. Snowball Ltd

This is a duplicate of the documents retained in our records. Please keep your copy in a safe place, it is important that it is produced so that saddle alterations, adjustments or re-flocking can be recorded.

We recommend that the saddle and the saddle fittings are checked at least twice a year. Horses frequently change shape through work, age etc. necessitating adaptions to the saddle.

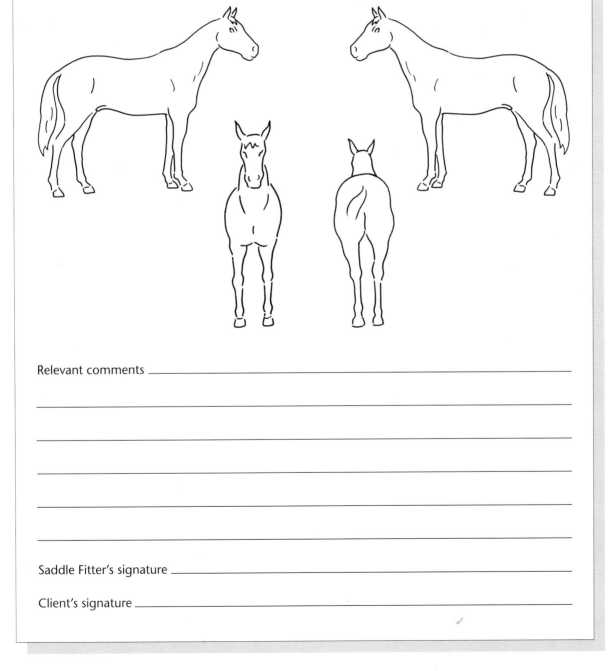

Relevant comments _____

_____

_____

_____

_____

Saddle Fitter's signature _____

Client's signature _____

132. The panel mark left after the horse has been ridden.

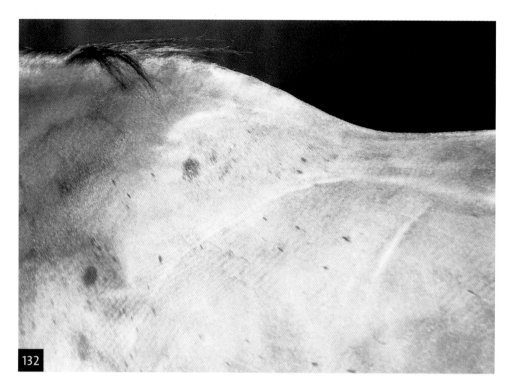

Although the specific guidance regarding subsequent checks will vary with individual cases, the client will always be advised to have the saddle checked in the near future, as it may require adjustment after several hours of riding. This necessity can, in fact, vary hugely depending upon the age, type and conformation of the horse and also the weight of the rider. Nevertheless, even if everything seems fine, the saddle should certainly be checked no later than six months after purchase – and it may be significantly sooner than that.

The rider should expect to pay for this service. Hopefully, if the saddler/ saddle fitter has a mobile workshop, any adjustments to the flocking can done on site. This is the most satisfactory procedure, and the most cost-effective from the client's perspective. However, if this is not possible, then the saddle will have to be returned to the workshop. It will then require refitting after the work and should not simply be sent back to the client or collected by the client from the workshop as this would, at best, involve guesswork. Obviously, however, this refitting involves significantly more time and effort and this will be reflected in the cost.

The following are true-life anecdotes that emphasize the importance of the saddle fitting certificate and the post-purchase check.

The first, which concerns a rare example of dishonesty, involved a saddle fitted by one of my staff. The client concerned telephoned and complained that, far from proving a good fit, the saddle was 'rubbing' and 'making the horse's back very sore'. Accepting that absolutely no one is totally infallible, I went myself to deal with the complaint.

The client, unnecessarily aggressive in manner, produced horse and saddle. The saddle certainly did not fit, being far too narrow for the horse (and I mean *far* too narrow) and I knew instantly that there was more to the story.

The client continued to rant and complain. When I asked to see her record of the fitting she replied that unfortunately it was lost! 'Don't worry', I said, 'I've brought our copy with me.' Body language told the story! Looking very awkward she said, 'I can't think all that's necessary – there's the horse, there's the saddle. You can see the results. We don't need records to prove how bad the fitting is.' I agreed wholeheartedly and she began to look very complacent. 'However', I said, 'I think we will just check what my saddle fitter recorded.' I then produced the trump card – the record of the actual fitting, including a full description of the horse – complete with the owner's signature. 'How strange', I said, 'the saddle was actually fitted for a 15.2 hands brown gelding and I would say that this horse is well over 16 hands – and surely he's a bay?'

All this was very unpleasant and time-wasting. There is absolutely no excuse for such dishonesty and I presented the lady concerned with an invoice for the time I had wasted on a non-existent problem. I discovered later that, almost immediately after buying the saddle, she unexpectedly sold the little brown gelding for which it had been fitted. The new owner didn't want to purchase the saddle – and the lady concerned thought that she could cheat her way into acquiring a new saddle for her bay horse. Ninety-nine per cent of clients are honest, but then there's the other one per cent.

The second case again concerns a saddle that had been fitted by one of my staff. Some three months after the initial fitting, the owner complained that the mare had become very sensitive, put her ears back at the sight of the saddle, was generally irritable and far less willing than previously.

The mare was in her stable when I arrived and I asked for her to be stood up outside her box so that I could examine her back. I found that she was sensitive in several areas, most especially at the base of the withers. The owner fetched the offending saddle from the tack room and, sure enough, at the sight of it the mare flattened her ears – but she needn't have worried, I didn't need to put the saddle on to determine the cause of the problem. The saddle was far too wide and undoubtedly creating several pressure points. I pointed this out to the owner and then asked her to produce her copy of the saddle fitting record. 'I'll run and get it', she said – or words to that effect. She obviously appreciated that the record was an important document – but she patently hadn't made use of the information it contained! In block letters my member of staff had written, 'The mare is very seriously overweight and the saddle will need to be refitted two or three times – and may even need to be changed as she becomes fitter.' (I should explain that saddle fitters prefer to fit a saddle when the horse is in regular work and in reasonable condition, but there are some circumstances when this isn't possible and then the fit of the saddle will inevitably need more frequent checking than is usual).

I took a pattern of the withers and measured the mare's girth – and then compared the measurements with those taken when the saddle had originally been fitted. The difference was even more that I'd expected, indicating just how gross the mare must have been. On this occasion, bearing in mind the fitter's original note, we changed the saddle free of any extra charge.

The Delights and Drawbacks of a Bespoke Saddle

I should say from the start that I usually try to discourage clients from commissioning made-to-measure saddles! *Very occasionally*, the only way to achieve the 'right' answer does involve making a bespoke saddle – but it is a route down which I prefer not to tread, because it can be fraught with problems.

Before elaborating, there is one very important fact to which I should alert all horse owners. The term 'made-to-measure' is often used very loosely nowadays. Traditionally the process of making a bespoke saddle involved the following steps.

1. Discussions taking place with regard to what the rider wanted to achieve from the saddle, the preferred type and style, the type and colour of the leather, etc. The needs of the rider would be fully discussed but the horse, as always, would be the first consideration.

2. Several trees would be tried on the horse's back (see photo 133), the selection made being dependent on the horse's conformation, the rider's shape and size and the discipline for which the saddle was needed. At around this point, before any significant working of materials was begun, a substantial deposit would be paid by the client.

3. Patterns of the flap shape, etc., would be taken to facilitate establishing the length of the rider's leg, riding position, etc.

4. An interim fitting would probably take place to ensure correct panel shape and fit. At the same time the saddler would have verified that the cosmetic appeal of the saddle would match the rider's expectations.

5. When the saddle was completed a final fitting would take place and any adjustments needed would be made. At this point the rider would 'try' the saddle and it would be hoped that it fulfilled expectations. That being the case, the balance due to the saddler would be paid.

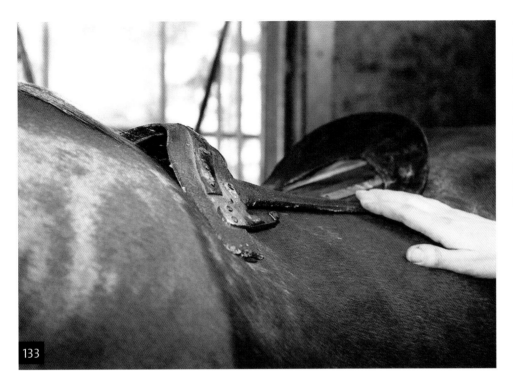

133. Any truly bespoke saddler will start by trying different saddle trees on the horse's back to choose a suitable base on which to construct a correctly fitting saddle. A bare tree can be checked thoroughly to ensure that it follow the contours and conformation of the horse's back before a panel is designed that is suitable for both horse and rider.

This traditional method of producing bespoke saddles is now often replaced by the making of template patterns, according to which the saddle is then produced by one of the large Walsall manufacturers. Excellent as all these services may be, they do not fulfil the original definition of 'made-to-measure'. Interim fittings are impractical in these circumstances and are actually deemed unnecessary because the saddle is being made exactly to template. This means there is no opportunity to see the part-made saddle on the horse and for the client to be assured that the finished article will fill expectations.

So, why are bespoke saddles required? On *very, very rare occasions* they may be necessary to accommodate some physical abnormality in the horse. Occasionally, a special saddle is needed to fulfil a particular style – sometimes to match up with an existing saddle. As an example, a bespoke saddle might be required by a rider involved in display work, who needs a realistic copy of a particular type of historic saddle. These exceptional circumstances aside, it is important to understand that few horses are actually difficult to accommodate with a saddle that fits. It is a total myth that a large percentage of horses cannot be equipped 'off the peg'. Of course, the ability to equip a wide variety of horses and ponies of varying breeds, heights, sizes and types – for all the various disciplines – pre-supposes that the retailer/ saddle fitter concerned has a stock of several hundreds of saddles. When this is the case, the chances are that the horse or pony can almost always be fitted from stock – albeit that providing the very best possible fit may involve some adjustments to the panels or similar to comply with the idiosyncrasies of the particular animal.

Despite these facts, however, the majority people who want a saddle made especially for their horse do so because of their perception that the finished saddle will provide the ultimate 'perfect' fit. The reality is often a disappointment. Not because the saddle has been poorly crafted...not because the saddle fitter has fallen down on the job...

In answer to the obvious question, 'Why, then?', I will elaborate on what I term the 'hidden dangers' of the bespoke saddle that is produced to templates.

The saddle fitter will take all the necessary measurements. A series of templates will be made using a flexicurve across the horse's back, starting an inch behind the withers. Similar patterns will be taken of side elevations of the spine. (Occasionally, it is suggested that the horse's owner takes and supplies the saddler with the measurements. I would strongly recommend against this practice because it is all too easy to get it wrong!) The type and style of the saddle will obviously be discussed. The owner will be provided with a wide choice of leathers in a variety of colours. The saddle fitter will take the utmost care to interpret the needs of the horse and the preferences of the rider – BUT IT CAN STILL GO WRONG!

Sometimes, the saddle will then be made in the retailer's own workshop, but more often than not the measurements and information will be sent to one of the large saddle manufacturers, many of whom offer excellent specialist services. BUT IT CAN STILL GO WRONG!

The turn-around time for made-to-measure saddles varies considerably but, allowing for the fact that most well-founded saddle makers have full order books, it is rarely less than several weeks. During this time, the horse's shape may have altered considerably, especially in the case of a youngster who has been involved in a constructive schooling programme since the measurements were originally taken. I should emphasize that, provided the measurements were followed precisely, it is very unlikely that the finished article won't be absolutely satisfactory in every way, in terms of construction. But, if the horse has changed shape in the meantime, the process has still, in one major respect, GONE WRONG.

Here is a true story. A Master Saddler friend of mine in the South of England, one of the few left who does make saddles to measure starting with the tree fitting etc., was embarrassed to have a complaint levelled against him by the owner of one of the specially made saddles, who said that it was 'not well made, did not fit the horse and was not comfortable' – and in addition, 'was too expensive'! I have known this saddler personally for many years; he is a wonderful craftsman, a man of absolute integrity and honour and, as you can imagine, he was pretty miffed at this complaint. So I went along to try to mediate and bring the matter to a civilized and amicable conclusion.

The saddle was beautifully made; it fitted the horse absolutely perfectly; it matched the original specification precisely. The problem was simply that the client found it uncomfortable. The mid-brown colour, selected from the leather samples shown at the inception, was identical to the sample. But the client now thought that this particular brown did not do her chestnut horse 'justice'. However, to make the complaint go away, the saddler gave the client her money back, I sold the client another saddle 'off the peg' which she liked, approved of the colour and found comfortable. I gave the profit of the transaction to the original saddler – problem solved.

So, what's to be learnt from this? No matter how good a job the saddler did, no matter how well it fitted the horse, no matter how correct the colour chosen from the original sample, the poor old saddler had to give the money back and was left with a saddle, no longer new, that was made specifically for a particular client. He had lost money and possibly (knowing how rumour spreads in the horse world) suffered damage to his reputation. And why? Just because the saddle was not deemed 'comfortable' by a client unable to try it in the first place. And here we have a 'chicken and egg' situation. How can you possibly know how comfortable a saddle is until is has been made? The final irony here is that, after all this wasted hard work and fuss, the client was completely satisfied with a saddle 'off the peg'!

Despite all the difficulties that can arise with bespoke saddles there are – *occasionally* – circumstances in which a made-to-measure saddle is the only practical solution. Earlier in this chapter I mentioned an example of a horse with an exceptionally dipped back, for whom a saddle was built successfully on a 'banana' tree. Here is another example of bespoke saddle making...

I like to boast that my company's stock of saddles, usually averaging seven or eight hundred, is sufficiently large and diverse to cater for virtually all the horses and ponies I am called upon to fit and – as will be evident from the previous pages – I perpetually preach that very few horses are genuinely difficult to provide with a suitable saddle. I stand by these comments – but the 'very few' do exist!

I was recently called out to fit a general purpose saddle for a horse used in battle enactment activities. The inquiry originated on the telephone and his owner promptly answered all my questions. After a general description I was informed that the horse was well over 18 hands, very broad across the withers and 'substantial through the girth'. I have to admit to thinking that the owner was exaggerating the horse's size. Not a bit of it – if anything he'd downscaled the measurements quite substantially! Don't run away with the idea that this was an unattractive hulk – far from it – but I for one wouldn't want to face this magnificent animal in a battle charge! The saddle was (necessarily) specially made and I am happy to report that it fitted beautifully. While the vast majority of horses can be fitted 'off the peg', there is a minority of vast horses who cannot!

Buying a Horse with Tack

A moment's diversion here to look at a practice that, on the one hand, can mirror the satisfaction of acquiring the perfect bespoke saddle and, on the other hand, can represent disaster. Just before writing this book, when giving a talk to a branch of the Pony Club, I was asked, 'What do you think about buying a pony complete with tack?' The simple answer is – if the tack fits – brilliant! If it doesn't fit – disaster! I have seen excellent tack, that has been maintained in superb condition, acquired in this way. I have also seen instances where tack, which doesn't even remotely fit, has been deliberately sold to first-time buyers – a very mean trick. The more comprehensive answer to the question thus lies in persuading the seller to allow the saddle fitting to be checked by a Qualified Saddle Fitter before all the money is handed over!

(Especially where children are concerned, although the way the saddle fits the pony must take priority, it is also important that the child finds it comfortable and that it is suitable for the child's experience and the types of riding envisaged.)

CHAPTER 4

Common Fitting Problems and Solutions

I SHOULD EMPHASIZE that, in this chapter, I am no longer talking about ill-fitting saddles as such, but about the practical problems that can arise when accommodating horses of unusual conformation and movement. As a starting point, I am assuming that the saddle in question has initially been properly fitted and passes all the seven static tests mentioned in Chapter 3 (the possible exception being the saddle with an 'overactive' rear panel, discussed later). However, just because a saddle fulfils all the static criteria, it does not necessarily follow that when the horse is ridden it will sit in perfect balance laterally, fore and aft, and will not move or swing. In fact, there will inevitably be *some* movement because, as the horse moves through the various figures and gaits, he will flex and bend, and any rigid or semi-rigid structures attached to his back will move in sympathy – to a lesser or greater degree. The trained saddle fitter will, of course, know just how much movement is acceptable and will make judgements and recommendations accordingly. Thus, what is being sought is a basically well-fitting saddle that moves as little as possible but it may, in some cases, still be necessary to find a means of reducing this movement further. Common problems that may require such a remedy are as follows.

Saddle Moving Forward

Generally speaking, saddles move forward most readily on Arabs, Cobs and native breeds with very little in respect of withers and fairly flat backs, whose back profile tends to be wide, extra wide or extra, extra wide. This tendency is compounded if, as is often the case, the animal is croup-high (see photo 99, page 60) and/or has no hollow at all behind the scapulae. Any movement of the saddle forward will, of course, become most evident in downward transitions or when jumping.

There are four common remedies used to counteract this problem.

The Point Strap. This is a girth billet strap attached to the point of the saddle tree (see photo 93, page 57). It is often found as a standard fitment on showing and dressage saddles and is very common now on saddles made for specific breeds which are likely to have wide, extra wide or extra, extra wide trees. The use of this strap tends to vastly improve the problem of a saddle moving forward and probably works well at least 80 per cent of the time. It does, however, bring with it a potential problem insofar as the addition of this strap at an appropriate girth pressure can often lead to a lifting of the back of the saddle. Thus most of the well-designed saddles fitted with point straps, or which incorporate them as subsequent modifications, will also incorporate a balance strap. These two outer straps, used together, will often stop a saddle going forward and reduce live or excessive movement of the rear panels. There are now girths on the market which have offset buckles (see photo 136, page 95) to help with the lie of the girth and these supplementary straps under the rider's leg.

The Fore-girth. Sometimes, in the most extreme cases, a fore-girth has to be used as a last resort. This is effectively rather like a small anti-cast roller placed onto the horse and girthed up immediately behind the elbows before the saddle is fitted and this is a considerable physical barrier to prevent saddles from going forward. However, some horses just can't tolerate this arrangement and often a horse wearing a fore-girth will perform far less well than he should, particularly in downward transitions. There are fore-girths available which do not employ a metal arch, but these tend to work rather less well, even though they are patently more comfortable for the horse.

The Crupper. I am bound to say that I think this particular invention is little short of barbaric and, happily, it is rarely seen nowadays. It is most often employed on very small ponies, although it is also a common accessory to Spanish and Portuguese saddles (photo 77, page 47). In simple terms, it is a strap attached at one end to the back of the saddle (usually via a metal ring), while the other end of the strap fits under the pony's tail in a soft hoop. Plainly, the saddle cannot move forward because it is simply anchored to the underside of the animal's tail, but I have seen the undersides of tails rubbed raw by such devices.

The Anti-slip Pad. There are many anti-slip pads on the market. They tend to be rubber or synthetic pads (see photo 134), either panel-shaped only or entirely saddle-shaped, and they may feel slightly sticky to the touch. These can be exceedingly effective initially, but the efficacy does tend to wane with wear. *If these pads are very thick, they can and do substantially change the fit of a saddle so, if they are to be used, the saddles should be fitted correctly with them in place.*

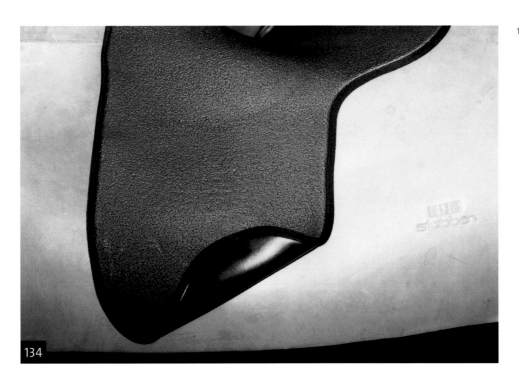

134. An anti-slip pad.

Saddle Moving Back

When saddles move back it is almost always a problem of conformation. The horse may have very large or exaggerated movement, work heavily on the forehand, or have a well-muscled front with the physique trailing off behind – what some people describe as 'wasp-waisted'. The anti-slip pad as described in the last section may assist in such cases but it is rather more likely that a breast plate or breast girth will be used. I prefer the use of the hunting breast plate as, in my experience, this works pretty well and it is cosmetically more appealing than the breast girth, which can also inhibit forward movement. In this respect, I am constantly surprised by how often the latter are used on racehorses.

Saddle Moving to One Side

This can be a massive problem. It is almost always the result of one shoulder being considerably larger than the other or, in the earlier stages, of the horse simply not bending round the rider's leg in one direction (being one-sided). This initial one-sidedness may be the result of undiagnosed injury, or inherent in that particular horse but, if the condition is not addressed, it will inevitably worsen.

Since one-sidedness presents a major challenge to the saddle fitter, and will compromise a horse's performance in any discipline, it is worthwhile looking at this problem in some detail.

Pick up any equestrian magazine and somewhere in the contents you can pretty much rely on finding reference to the straightness of the horse. We all know the maxim 'ride the horse forward, ride him straight' and yet everyone recognizes the fact that no horse is born straight and that the most skilful riders, who have absolute straightness as a long-term ideal, rarely, if ever, achieve it. The vast majority of horses, even those who are well ridden, fall some way short of total straightness and, by definition, are not muscled up completely symmetrically. This lack of straightness in the horse is compounded by a similar situation in the rider. How many people are totally ambidextrous? Virtually everyone 'favours' one side or the other; very few riders sit perfectly square and most have a dominant hand and leg. Any crookedness in the rider will have some effect on the horse's way of going, and when a significantly crooked rider is paired with an already crooked horse the impact can be substantial.

This is not to say that every case of asymmetry is a product of errant riding. Sometimes, for example, a sacroiliac injury can lead a horse to pull on one side of the forehand much more than the other, thereby developing much more shoulder definition on one side. Similarly, horses who have been, or still are, used for driving will often have uneven shoulders, especially if regular hill work is involved. What happens is that, when pulling a load, or bracing against it, the horse will tend to favour his naturally stronger side, thus adopting a slight sideways inclination, which encourages further uneven muscular development.

Although not confined to the horse's shoulders, asymmetry in that region is very common. While some owners are aware of the condition, it more often goes unrecognized until it is pointed out. Asymmetrical shoulders are, however, one of the first features that attract the attention of an experienced saddle fitter, because of the adverse effect on the saddle and the way it locates when the horse is being ridden. Basically, when the scapula on the over-developed side rotates, it will constantly push up against the front of the tree which, of course, pushes the saddle away diagonally to the other side of the horse (see photo 135). The problem will be compounded by the rider being uncomfortable and unable to sit centrally.

I have previously mentioned (in Chapter 3) the need for the saddle fitter to be conversant with the horse's movement and to examine the musculature before beginning the fitting process, but the saddle fitter's skills are tested further when fittings to significantly asymmetrical horses are undertaken. Since detailed analysis of the condition and finding the best solution will require seeing the horse being ridden and since, in a sense, all such fittings are 'remedial', let us examine this problem from the viewpoint of a saddle fitter who has actually been asked to carry out a remedial fitting. (Remedial fittings carried out for other reasons are discussed in the next chapter.)

The saddle fitter who arrives to check the fitting of an existing saddle can be faced with a dilemma. The basic fitting is acceptable – that is, the saddle is the correct size and width for the horse concerned. However, the horse has one shoulder noticeably larger than the other. The saddle fitter asks to see the horse ridden. The

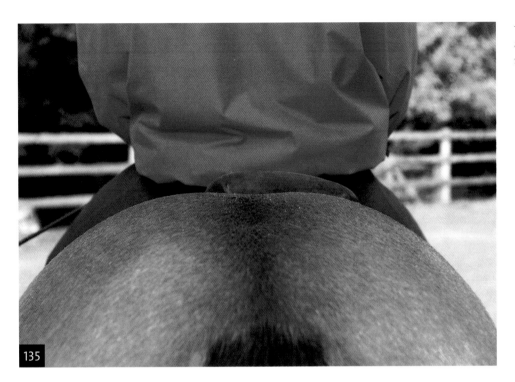

135. The effect of an asymmetrical horse on the saddle.

rider is seriously crooked; the horse's larger nearside shoulder is pushing the saddle off to the right. Is the lack of symmetry in the horse the result of a former injury, or has it resulted from poor schooling methods? Is the rider's seat inherently crooked, or was the rider previously located more or less centrally before being pushed off to the right because the saddle is being pushed over that way?

It is easier to note and diagnose this sort of problem in trot than in walk or canter because the horse trots on diagonal pairs, making the thrust of the larger shoulder far greater. Now the saddle fitter must attempt to decide where the basic cause lies and this, again, is an example of why the Society of Master Saddlers' saddle fitting qualification demands considerable understanding of the horse's anatomy and musculature.

In cases (which may require veterinary confirmation) where the cause of the asymmetry is an irreversible injury, astute and essentially permanent re-flocking will be necessary to accommodate the problem. Alterations to the panel and the provision of a balance strap may also be required. If the appropriate adjustments are not made the saddle will be unbalanced and thus likely to make the existing problem worse.

In cases where the asymmetry has been acquired or exacerbated by riding and schooling practices, there are two basic solutions. The first may help riders who are, themselves, crooked as a result of physical conditions. It may also suit the requirements of less experienced riders, especially those who have acquired older horses whose asymmetrical musculature and general way of going are well established. Essentially, in a procedure similar to that used on behalf of the permanently injured horse, a saddler can reduce the flocking or adjust the panel significantly so that the saddle accommodates the existing shape of the horse. Again, a balance strap may also help. In effect, this is a case of two 'crookeds' sitting the rider straight. While, as a rider, I tend to dislike this remedy (except where it assists those with physical conditions), as a saddle fitter, I must admit that it is sometimes very effective.

In cases where the client is able and willing to address acquired asymmetry in the horse through remedial schooling, any re-flocking of the saddle to reduce the unwanted movement should be seen as a temporary measure. In the short term, it will reduce the diagonal movement of the saddle and make it easier for the rider to sit squarely. From that starting point, the rider can embark on a programme of exercises which emphasize working the horse towards the side on which he has difficulty in bending. Carried out astutely, under instruction if necessary, these can be most effective on young horses (although the work should not be undertaken too vigorously, or muscle spasm, stiffness and resistances may result). On older horses progress may be slower because, as mentioned, their musculature and way of going are more established. However, such work should, in time, achieve a straighter horse and rider – at which point, the saddle will need refitting once more!

While we have looked at these problems of asymmetry primarily from the point of view of remedial fitting, in cases where a new saddle is to be supplied designs with air panels (see Chapter 1) are worth considering, since they allow for rapid adjustment by an experienced fitter. In cases where traditionally flocked saddles are supplied new, but require considerable adjustment to accommodate the horse's asymmetry, the arrangement becomes something akin to a bespoke fitting, and similar financial arrangements may be required.

Saddles with 'Overactive' Rear Panels

By this, I mean saddles which bounce up and down (especially in rising trot), or wave from side to side. Often this happens if the rear panels don't sit evenly, or have something of a banana shape. This can be down to the design, or simply too much flocking in the centre of the panel permitting a rocking movement. It is less likely to happen with rear panels that are fitted with gussets. However, girth straps mounted slightly in front of the point of balance can cause this unnecessary movement and again balance straps almost always completely eradicate the problem.

Subsidiary Equipment

To conclude this chapter, let us look at some other items of equipment which can either help or hinder the fitting of saddles.

Girths

A girth is obviously an essential item but, while a well-chosen one can provide optimum comfort for the horse and security for the rider, one that is ill-chosen or neglected can cause discomfort or even serious injury.

Leather girths often look beautiful and are superbly made, but if they are not looked after properly they can become very hard and crack, causing significant discomfort for the horse and even open wounds. It certainly true to say that a beautifully finished girth can look really smart in a showing class, but leather girths have been much superseded in recent years by synthetic girths of one sort or another.

Personally, I like synthetic girths made of very soft neoprene and I am particularly fond of the humane design (photo 136, left). In any event, as a general rule, thick girths are potentially more comfortable than very thin ones. Just imagine if you had an exceedingly thin belt pulled very tight around your waist – how much more comfortable would a thick belt be at the same tension?

Girths fitted with elastic inserts on one side (photo 136, centre) are an item of which I am wary. They are intended to accommodate significant expansion of the rib cage, as when the horse makes a big jumping effort or takes deep breaths during serious exertion. However, while girths of this type work perfectly well when new, after a few years (or even months) the elastic often becomes very tired and simply fails to do what it is supposed to do. In addition, if such a girth is used on an asymmetrical horse, not only will it fail to stop the saddle from going to one side, it will positively encourage this to happen if the elastic is used on the same side as the dominant shoulder.

Girth buckles without rollers are a pet hate of mine. It has never failed to astound me how often fairly expensive, beautifully made, leather girths are fitted

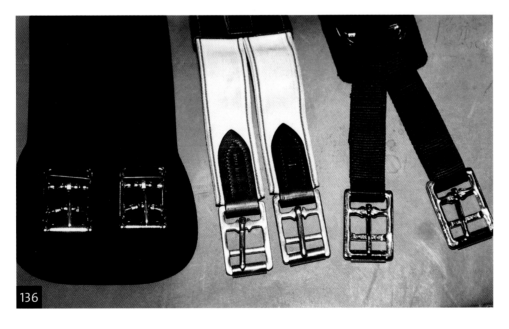

136. A selection of girths (left) soft synthetic, (centre) leather with elasticated inserts, (right) offset buckles.

with buckles without rollers. There can be simply no argument other than cost in favour of a roller-less buckle, and yet the difference in price between these and the type with buckles is only a few pence. When tight, roller-less buckles are hard to adjust and often cut into the billet strap, damaging and weakening the leather. Furthermore, nothing is quite so tiresome as trying to do up a girth on a horse who habitually 'blows out' and expands his rib cage than a buckle that does not run easily over the billet strap.

Numnahs and Pads

The word numnah originally described a saddle-shaped pad used to absorb sweat and provide some degree of protection for horses such as cavalry mounts, being ridden for long periods in arduous conditions, often in saddles that were not tailored to their individual needs. It is nowadays used loosely to describe all manner of good, bad and indifferent coverings placed between the horse's back and the saddle.

First of all, if a saddle fits correctly, it does not require significant padding of any sort to aid its performance. Certainly, a thin saddle cloth which looks smart and keeps the saddle clean can be used without affecting the saddle's fit at all. However, despite the progress mentioned in the Introduction, I still see saddles padded up with foam, large pads to the front or the rear, or just thick rugs intended to stop the saddle bearing down on to the horse's withers. Let me stress that there are very few horses who actually perform better with a numnah or some such added *if the saddle fits properly in the first place*. However, we live in the real world and some riders live very long distances from a saddler, so the use of such padding, whilst it can never be recommended, can sometimes and to some degree be excused. Therefore, let us look at some specific examples of padding.

The Front Riser. This is often used on a horse with high withers, or where there is substantial muscle wastage at each side of the trapezius area because the horse is in poor condition or very old. In the latter cases, what it sets out to do is simply fill in the gap left by the muscle wastage. Fitted and used with some care it can be effective if the saddle cannot take any further adjustment but, used carelessly or incorrectly, it will lift the front of the saddle beyond the position of correct balance, which will tend to throw the rider back to sit on the buttocks rather than the seat bones, with the lower legs too far forward.

The Rear Riser Pad. This is a device intended to correct a saddle that sits too low behind and its use assumes that the saddle cannot be adjusted by flocking in the rear panels (see photo 137). Again, where used, this needs very careful fitting as very frequently it encourages the saddle to bridge (for bridging, see photo 113, page 67) and if the horse has a dipped back it will certainly lead to severe pressure problems under the rear panel close to the lumbar area. It is very sad that, even at quite high level dressage competitions, one sees many riders use rear riser pads under their dressage squares – it has almost become a fashion item. Some riders appear to use these pads in an attempt to adjust their own posture so that their lower leg is further back in what they assume to be the 'classical' position. However, if the saddle was originally a good fit and in good balance, by doing this they risk creating unnecessary pressure on the horse's back and, indeed, tipping themselves forward into a 'fork seat'.

137. A rear riser pad. This item can have legitimate uses but requires careful fitting. Too often, nowadays, these pads are used for entirely inappropriate reasons.

Adjustable Air-filled Saddle Cloths. These devices encourage the rider to inflate either the front to emulate a front riser or the back to emulate a rear riser. In addition to the comments already made about these particular items, I am concerned that the uninitiated might not know when an air-filled saddle cloth is too heavily inflated. That said, the device does come with comprehensive instructions and I can see some merit in it under certain circumstances. However, I reiterate my main premise that it is better if saddles fit properly in the first place.

Restraining Tapes. These (see photo 138) are a really important factor when fitting numnahs and saddle pads if we expect them to remain in place for any length of time while the horse is performing in all gaits and jumping. In their most simple form, the front tapes fasten around the girth straps, with an additional loop on the bottom edge of the saddle cloth or square for the girth to thread through. One

138. Restraining tapes must be correctly positioned and of good quality.

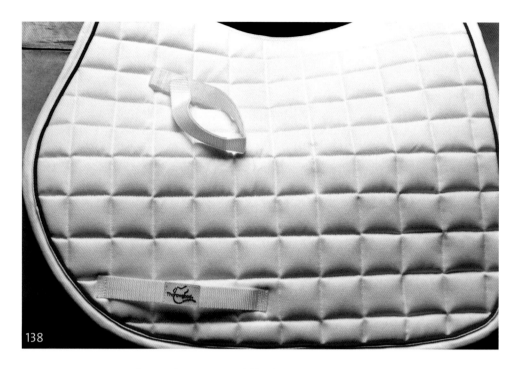

138

cautionary note – when selecting a saddle cloth or numnah, run your hand along the edging and make sure that it has been nicely finished and does not have the sharp or raw edge often found on the cheaper products, as this frequently shaves the horse's hair under this region and can cause soreness.

CHAPTER 5

'Holistic' Confusion and Remedial Fittings

In this chapter, I would like to discuss some of the misguided practices and assumptions that can give rise to problems with the fitting of saddles. I hope that the true stories recounted will help readers to avoid similar situations.

Interference, Overlap and Consultation

A great deal has been said – and written – about the need for a holistic approach to horses. In some cases 'holistic' has come to be redefined as 'interference' and associated with misunderstanding and intolerance. It has led to some professionals (more commonly, the self-appointed variety) attempting to take over the work of other professionals and has created confusion and misunderstanding, not least amongst horse owners. All of this is a great pity because a genuine exchange of knowledge and expertise would be immensely beneficial to all concerned.

There are a *few* professionals with a multiplicity of qualifications, skills and techniques – but it is very rare to find a vet who is also a qualified farrier, a BHS instructor who has been assessed and registered as a Qualified Saddle Fitter – and so on. While, for the benefit of the horse, there must be some helpful cross-consultation between the professions, that is quite different from take-over, which is dangerous. It all goes back to 'a little knowledge is a dangerous thing'.

Because I undertake a great many remedial fittings, I work in consultation with several vets, most of whom are equine specialists. However, not one of them would attempt to fit a saddle. Although several have an understanding of the basic principles, they are well aware that this is far removed from being able to undertake the actual selection and fitting.

In the same way, Qualified Saddle Fitters are required to be able to make an examination of the horse's back and to recognize tender, sore or damaged areas.

They must also be able to detect gait malfunctions, unlevelness and, indeed, the physical signs of the ageing process. 'Back problems', whether acute or chronic, will undoubtedly demand special consideration by the saddle fitter, as may certain root causes of gait abnormality. However, while saddle fitters should recommend that such conditions be referred for veterinary attention, it is not a fitter's business to make specific diagnosis, much less suggest a form of treatment.

I have explained this as the background to discussing two cases that arose shortly before writing this book. In the first, I was asked to undertake a remedial fitting for a horse who was displaying signs of unspecified back problems. Previously eager to please, good tempered and willing, he had become irritable and nappy. The vet had diagnosed soreness at the base of the withers and had suggested calling me in to examine the saddle. Just as well! It was far, far too narrow and must have been causing the animal considerable pain. The saddle had been supplied and 'fitted' by the owner's farrier – it happened to be one his wife wanted to sell. The farrier concerned enjoys an absolutely first-class reputation for his shoeing expertise – I just wish that he would restrict himself to farriery.

My second story involves a youngster who was being lunged in preparation for backing. All was going well until the instructor introduced the saddle. Then, on the three occasions he was saddled, the horse had turned himself completely inside out. Previously quiet and confident when handled by the owner, he had become tense and nervous.

The saddle had seen better days. The instructor explained that she had lent it 'because it was silly to risk a good saddle becoming damaged when the youngster was lunged'. It didn't take very long to discover that the saddle had a badly broken tree!

Very, very few young horses have a back problem. Quite a lot will develop one quite early in their careers – often as a direct result of someone's ignorance or irresponsibility. The instructor had intended to be helpful – but might have been the cause of a young horse going disastrously wrong. As it was, the youngster was turned away for a few weeks to give his back – and mind – time to recover. A young horse's back is very precious and demands infinite care and consideration – which must include fitting a saddle with extreme care.

(I would like to say, as an aside, how much I deplore the habit of lungeing a riderless, saddled horse. However well the saddle fits, there will inevitably be some movement when the horse is working on a circle – especially if the animal is fresh and playful. A lot of damage can be done in this way. A correctly fitted, properly adjusted roller is an infinitely better option. These comments do not, of course, apply to a horse being lunged with a rider.)

In this previous case, even though the instructor may have been rather thoughtless, and perhaps crossed the line of professional expertise, she was at least well intentioned. My next story is simply an example of woeful ignorance.

A young woman asked me to examine her saddle. It had been bought, across a retail counter no less, by her 'expert' – in this case a BHSAI. Apparently the saddle was slipping forward and, when the horse and rider were going down-hill and at anything other than a very sedate pace, it was actually sliding up the horse's neck. The instructor insisted that it was the rider's inability to sit still and square that was creating the problem and the young woman explained that she was no longer enjoying her riding, that she felt absolutely useless and almost wished she had never bought the horse. All in all, a sorry state of affairs!

The horse concerned had decidedly 'odd' conformation. He was very nar-row to the point of being almost pigeon-chested, his front legs came virtually 'out of one hole' and he had a back that was slightly roached. Let me add that he was aged, experienced, straightforward and seemed very kind and patient. He wasn't a 'looker' – but temperamentally he was just right as a first horse for a novice rider.

Experienced readers will be forming a picture and it won't take them long to establish that it wouldn't be easy to fit a saddle to a horse with this sort of conformation. The instructor had selected a saddle that was sufficiently wide to fit a 17 hand Warmblood and, at 18 inches, it was also far too long for this lightly built little horse who stood not much over 15 hands – and also too big for the petite rider. The rider explained gravely that her instructor had informed her that far too many horses were fitted with saddles that were too narrow. Her reasons for selecting such a large saddle also apparently related to her observing that the rider would 'feel more secure if the saddle was nice and big'.

The only thing about this remedial fitting that actually surprised me was that this first-time novice owner had managed to ride in it at all! I did get the problem sorted but, not surprisingly, the retail saddlery from which the orig-inal saddle had been purchased refused to give a refund. I took the saddle in part exchange but the rider was still out of pocket in a completely unneces-sary way. The instructor lost a client as a result of her faux pas because the rider, not surprisingly, had lost confidence in her judgement. If only she had-n't interfered in an aspect of horse management about which she clearly had absolutely no knowledge!

I suppose there are degrees of stepping outside one's area of expertise. One really wouldn't expect a carpet fitter to fit a saddle – especially one whose knowledge of horses was limited to giving a mint to his girlfriend's Cob! The owner explained, very seriously, that she had thought that someone used to measuring up, cutting and laying carpet should find fitting a saddle a complete doddle. She couldn't, she said, decide where it had all gone wrong but her horse was 'sensitive' along his back and 'put his ears back when I saddle him up'.

This was not surprisingly really – when you realize that the measurements carefully taken by the carpet fitter hadn't taken account of the need to provide a saddle with the largest possible bearing surfaces, so that weight is distributed over the greatest possible area of the horse's back. He had, quite literally, taken the measurements so as to provide as snug a fit as possible. The result was that the arch was pressing onto the base of the withers and the clearance along the gullet was totally inadequate. Once again, the saddle has been bought over the counter of a local saddlery. The rider had thought she would be saving money, but ended up losing quite a lot. It didn't help when I explained that most Qualified Saddle Fitters do not make a charge for fitting new saddles!

All for One and One for All – or Not!

I would not wish to give the impression that all of my remedial visits have to do with inappropriate professional overlap. There are many other causes of problems, one being that the old Musketeer's slogan of 'all for one and one for all' just doesn't work with saddles.

One such case concerns a horse who had developed a very sensitive area below the base of the withers. I was called in as a consultant by the owner's vet who was finding it difficult to fathom the cause of the problem.

The saddle had not been fitted by a Society of Master Saddlers Qualified Saddle Fitter, but I knew the individual concerned to be knowledgeable and professional and so I arrived doubting that I would find a problem with the saddle. However, there was – but not of the saddle fitter's making!

The horse looked well and in good condition. He was pretty evenly muscled up (absolutely no horse has totally symmetrical musculature) and yet the left-hand saddle panel had adopted a very strange shape. I was mystified – until I saw the owner's other horse! 'Do you by any chance use the saddle on this horse too?' I asked. 'Yes – he's retired from competition but my mother exercises him every day and it's the only saddle she finds comfortable.'

Problem solved. The aged horse was chronically one-sided as a result of an injury caused by a nasty fall across country that had put a premature end to his eventing career. I explained that a saddle quickly adopts any eccentricities in a horse's shape and that this was one reason why saddles should never be shared. I pointed out how the contours of the saddle had adapted to the shape of the former event horse and how pressure points were thus created when the saddle was used on the younger horse. I later discovered that the saddle had been fitted eighteen months previously, after which the owner had failed to arrange any saddle fitting checks. Far too long!

The owner would have saved herself a lot of time, trouble and money if she had restricted the use of the saddle to the horse for which it was fitted – and organized subsequent fitting checks. Incidentally, a saddle should, *ideally*, be used only by the rider whose physique and needs had been considered by the saddle fitter. While this may not always be entirely practical, it is a principle that should be given due consideration and it applies more and more as saddle design becomes increasingly innovative and individualistic.

My next story has similarities and concerns a referral from another vet. The horse had been bought for a teenage girl as a potential eventer. The same vet had carried out the pre-purchase veterinary inspection and, at the time, had not detected any problems. Now the horse was tender in an area corresponding with the back of the saddle. The vet was fairly certain that the saddle was at fault but wanted an opinion from a Qualified Saddle Fitter. Easy! The saddle just didn't fit. The tree was the wrong shape for the horse and was consequently not balanced. It was sitting substantially 'uphill', directly creating a great deal of highly undesirable pressure under the back of the saddle.

I discovered that the saddle had never been fitted for this particular horse but had been kept when the teenager's first horse was sold on. The parents (incidentally, both rode and were generally knowledgeable) thought that the saddle would be perfectly OK because both horses were just about 16 hands and had similar conformation!

Every saddle should be fitted to the individual horse. This is particularly important when the saddle has been used previously or bought second-hand. The saddle will have adapted to the shape of the original horse and, even when the basic fitting is acceptable, it is likely to need re-flocking.

Shape-shifting

The point made in the above story that the teenager's parents were generally quite knowledgeable brings me to another observation. There is a wide variation in owners' understanding of the reasons why a horse's profile may be subject to (sometimes quite dramatic) change, and also a tendency to confuse skeletal conformation with transitory 'shape'. While the skeletal structure of a three-year-old will remain basically unaltered into adulthood, he can be expected to 'grow' considerably as he matures and strengthens. Furthermore, the 'shape' of a horse, in terms of musculature and proportion of body fat, can vary a great deal according to the way he is managed, ridden and schooled.

A horse, for example, who is not ridden through from behind will not be correctly muscled up and will lack top line. Horses who work with their heads in the air – substantially above the bit – will be hollow-backed and also lacking in top line muscle. Horses who work on the forehand often develop particularly big shoulders while, at the same time, their quarters may be undeveloped. Those turned away on unrestricted early-season grass can become very fat and flabby, making it well-nigh impossible for them to work correctly until they lose the excess fat – and so on....

Here are two examples of clients who had a good – and a not so good – grasp of the effects of shape on saddle fitting.

In the first case the horse, although a very good type, was 'upside down' as a result of the way he had been ridden by his previous owner. The new owner, an extremely experienced rider, intended to re-school him and I could see that, with systematic training, his musculature would be transformed. Fortunately, because the new owner was an experienced horsewoman and stable manager, she was well aware that the new saddle would probably need to be adapted two or even three times during the re-training period.

Shortly after that visit, I was asked to refit a saddle for a Cob who had been turned out on too much, too rich grazing. I went to see the animal, taking with me the records and notes that had been completed at the time of the initial sale. I found that the saddle was now slipping – fairly badly. The horse was sensitive at the base of the withers and he most definitely had a small gall!

I followed up my examination by producing the records and notes made by my saddler at the time of the sale – in line with correct practice, the client had been given a copy to retain. I made a pattern of the withers and used a body tape to identify the horse's current shape and asked the client to compare my findings with the measurements taken on the day of the sale. I also read her the notes: 'Horse grossly overweight and should be in slow work for at least six weeks. Saddle will probably need adjusting after about four weeks. Suggest the use of a sheepskin girth sleeve to discourage galling.' The client assured me that she had carefully filed her copy of the record – but had failed to read it! She was very apologetic, but that wasn't quite the point and, indeed, things became more complicated.

Since the Cob was bloated in the extreme I suggested that the owner put him steadily back into work by lungeing him each day for at least two weeks while, at the same time, keeping him off the grass. The owner then insisted that she had real difficulty in understanding that the saddle, fitted while the Cob was in his original gross condition, would undoubtedly need adjustment as he began to gain muscle and lose fat!

Surely, people who adopt some form of dieting and/or exercise regime don't expect their original clothes to fit well if they're successful in losing a reasonable amount of weight, and it must be the same with horses and ponies.

Reverting to my earlier observation that people who are quite knowledgeable do not always put this knowledge into practice, here is a story about a really skilled and genuinely concerned rider who, nevertheless, 'missed a trick'.

A while ago, I was asked to give a second opinion about a saddle fitted by another saddle fitter – one not registered by the Society of Master Saddlers. The horse, a five-year-old, had been bought as a potential eventer. Just over 16 hands, perhaps a little too light in condition, he had a good eye and a co-operative attitude. The owner was convinced that the saddle was too narrow and was beginning to pinch. I asked why the original saddle fitter had not been called in to examine the saddle and was told it was because the owner had lost confidence in her ability.

It took me only two minutes to ascertain that the saddle was definitely too narrow and that, yes, it was beginning to pinch. While I was carrying out my examination the horse's owner, (obviously experienced, because she had taken two other horses up to Advanced level), explained the circumstances in which she had bought the latest acquisition. Apparently, he had been some-thing of a rescue case. Then rising four, he had been bought as a first horse. Just backed, he was far too quick and unpredictable for the novice owner and had begun to get nappy and difficult. Finally, the young woman concerned gave up trying to cope and turned him out into a nearly bare field. The pres-ent owner had passed that particular field at regular intervals and noticed him getting poorer and poorer. Finally, she managed to locate the then owner, who explained the circumstances – apparently saying she wanted him off her hands and inviting an offer. A trivial sum then exchanged hands. What had been potentially a nice seven-eighths bred horse – but was now a disaster in the making – was given a new home and a second chance.

Although the horse was in very poor condition, the new owner decided to put him into light work immediately. She explained 'Apparently he had begun to rear, run backwards and be generally nappy. I wanted to start him off quietly just for a few minutes each day while he was still very unfit and less likely to put up too many fights.' In experienced hands, the horse was now proving himself to be both talented and co-operative.

'Did you not realize that the horse, although still a little light, has obvi-ously built up a lot since you bought him and that the saddle fitted then would at least need adapting, even possibly exchanging?', I asked. The client admitted she hadn't stopped to consider the reasons why the saddle was quite obviously beginning to pinch.

Courtesy demanded that I suggest the original saddle fitter involved should be contacted and the owner agreed. When I telephoned the saddle fitter concerned she explained the circumstances in which the saddle had been fitted and said she wasn't remotely surprised that, if the horse's condition had improved, the saddle was starting to pinch. I asked if she had kept a record of the transaction, including a pattern of the withers and girth measurement, and the answer was 'No'. She was very lucky because, in this case, a dispute wasn't in question.

This saddler may have been slack in her record-keeping, and perhaps in not making the point that an early post-purchase check would have been appropriate in this case. However, she was not in error insofar as the saddle had been a satisfactory fit on the day that it was provided. Here, indeed, is a story that highlights the importance of providing a saddle giving the best-possible fitting on the day it's fitted. In this case, it demonstrates the other side of the coin.

The animal concerned was an aged Thoroughbred. She had been shown in Lightweight Hunter classes with considerable success. Later, she was used as a brood mare and produced seven foals. Like quite a lot of mares who have had several foals, her back was slightly dipped. She was also dropping away around the area of the withers, something that tends to happen to ageing Thoroughbreds, no matter how careful their management.

This mare had been fitted with a saddle that was far too wide. The resulting unwanted space had been filled up by inserting two layers of foam at the front of the saddle. The saddle fitter had said that these should be removed as the mare's shape improved. The mare was twenty-three years old and in very light work! (Just in case any queries arise in readers' minds, this particular saddle fitter was not a member of the Society of Master Saddlers.)

A saddle that is too wide can create just as many problems as one that is too narrow. Inserting pieces of foam may well exacerbate rather than cure the problem and this mare was being pinched every time she took a step forward.

I will reiterate that, while an experienced saddle fitter will endeavour to take into consideration likely future changes in the horse's shape, the fact remains that the saddle fitted must be that which best corresponds to the horse's shape *on the day of the fitting*. In this particular case, two errors of judgement occurred. First, the mare's shape was extremely unlikely to change drastically. Second, it is very unwise to insert pieces of foam or similar padding under any parts of the saddle. Doing so will almost certainly unbalance the saddle and so create pressure points – as in the case of this mare.

Lest it be thought that my entire existence is spent in visiting yards to sort out difficulties and disputes, let me end this chapter with a couple of more pleasant anecdotes.

First, while I was aware that a lot of the horses and ponies who compete in three-day driving trials are schooled astride, I've rarely been asked to fit saddles for them and so I looked forward to a rare visit to a driving yard. The yard's owner, who is very eminent in driving circles, had called me out to fit saddles for a pair of ponies driven by a client. The ponies were immaculately presented, well mannered and obedient. I was amazed by how responsive they were to the owner's voice and it was a pleasure to see the willing effort they put into their work. 'Horses for courses' – without doubt they were in the right job.

If fitting saddles to driving ponies is a rarity, checking a saddle fitting for a donkey is, so far, a one-off experience. And no, I don't mean 'donkey' as a derogatory term for a horse with less-than-average looks and ability but a real, live, long-eared donkey. These animals are reputedly stubborn, idle and difficult. I can only report that this charming donkey had the sweetest personality. She came to the gate the moment she was called (Rosie – a fitting name for a charming animal), was safely ridden by a very small child and driven to a tiny Governess Cart by the little girl's grandmother. A new experience for me and one I shall recall with pleasure.

CHAPTER 6

Responsibilities of Saddle Fitting

IN THIS BRIEF CHAPTER, I would like to draw on a number of points that have been made in detail elsewhere, to offer a summary of what should be expected of and by those involved in the saddle fitting process.

The Saddle Fitter's Responsibility to the Client

Professional saddle fitters should not regard themselves, nor be regarded by clients, as saddle salesmen. If the job of saddle fitting is undertaken with integrity and responsibility, in the way described in this book, the correct saddle will usually select itself by a process of elimination.

The saddle fitter should never seek to gloss over any areas of inadequacy and all advantages and disadvantages should be brought to the attention of the client. If, as often happens, the client has a preconceived idea of make or model which is simply inappropriate for the horse concerned, the saddle fitter must be resolute in making sure that the client understands this. Buying (or selling!) a saddle by label or reputation is simply not the right course of action.

The saddle fitter must take account of all relevant factors such as the horse's age and condition and how likely he is to change shape in the short term, and ensure that the saddle provided has adequate adjustment for any horse who is very young, very old, too fat or too thin, as it is tiresome for a client to have to change the saddle after a short time because it is no longer appropriate for the horse's current shape, condition and conformation. If the saddle provided is of the close-contact type, having little or no facility for reasonable adjustment, this must be stressed.

The saddle fitter must take profiles and weight tape measurements of the horse at the time of the fitting and make such other notes as are pertinent. A copy of this information will be provided to the client after the initial transaction. This provides mutual protection of the interests of both saddle fitter and client if the horse changes shape beyond all reasonable predictions, and will often save any disagreement or bad feeling in the future.

The client should be informed of recommended servicing durations and, if a saddle is altered or re-flocked, the altered saddle should always be fitted to the horse and not simply returned to the client by post or courier.

The Client's Responsibility to the Saddle Fitter

It will assist the saddle fitter greatly if all the preliminary information supplied in respect of the horse, the rider and the rider's requirements is as complete and accurate as possible.

At the time of the initial fitting, the horse should be presented to the saddle fitter in a clean, tidy manner and in a safe environment. The client or handler should be proficient in horse management and thus able to stand the horse up straight, and walk and trot him out actively. The client should also make the saddle fitter aware of any idiosyncrasies or vices the horse may have, such as kicking, biting or rearing, and also of any previous injuries, unevenness or unsoundness, particularly those associated with the horse's back or girth area. Similarly, if the horse is not yet fully broken, or only arrived recently and is an unknown quantity, the saddle fitter should be informed.

When the horse is being ridden, the saddle fitter will expect the rider to wear a safety hat, as it would be unreasonable to expect the saddle fitter to accept any responsibility whatsoever for an injury sustained while trying a new saddle if the rider was not properly equipped. It is a sad reflection that many professional riders habitually ride without safety helmets or back protectors.

CHAPTER 7

Some Observations of a Saddle Fitter

I WOULD LIKE TO CONCLUDE this book by commenting on a few issues that may have an impact on the preservation of saddlery and on the welfare of horse and rider.

First, I would like to recommend far greater use of mounting blocks! Often disparaged and regarded as the exclusive requisite of the less-than-agile, they are nowadays found in very few yards. This is a pity and the reason behind it is a gross misconception. Mounting from the ground will almost inevitably involve the saddle being dislodged and pulled to the left, at least to some extent – and often quite substantially. Occasionally, I see riders gyrating in the saddle with the girth still done up in an effort to relocate it! Not surprisingly, the horse concerned is none too happy – and I have actually seen one attempt to lie down in an effort get rid of the discomfort. Regular mounting from the ground, however athletic and supple the rider, is not good for the horse's back and may be the cause of physical and/or behavioural problems. It may also result in the saddle becoming twisted. If the girth slips badly, or a buckle fails, the rider may end up on the ground beneath a startled horse! I would like, therefore, to see solidly made mounting blocks (not upturned milk crates) strategically positioned to encourage their use in every yard. It is a strange phenomenon that many thinking riders, who are extremely considerate of their horse's welfare in other respects, fail to make use of this important piece of equipment.

My second point is that, almost every day, I see saddles balanced on top of stable doors or in equally unsuitable locations. Almost as often, I see saddles that are scratched or damaged, often in the cantle area, as a result of falling or being dropped. Cosmetically, this is very unattractive but, much more importantly, it isn't necessarily possible to determine any internal damage – such as a broken or cracked tree – without opening the saddle up.

Another cause for concern is the number of horses I see saddled up and left loose in the stable – a sure invitation to get down to roll. If dropping a saddle may damage it, imagine what being rolled on by a horse might do! If it has been dropped or rolled on, or if the saddled horse has fallen, the saddle should be checked by a professional saddler before it is used again. Although this is a charge-able service (and major repairs may, in some cases, prove costly), it must be seen as an essential safety and welfare matter.

Finally, a word about lungeing. Throughout this book, I have said that eques-trian professionals should concentrate on their own particular areas of expertise, so it might seem out of place for me to comment on what might be regarded as a form of schooling. However, I am not concerned here with the niceties of work-ing the horse impeccably on the lunge, but simply with safe practice.

My work often involves me watching a horse being lunged, and the way this is done ranges from the highly professional, through ineffectual to downright dan-gerous. Might I please, therefore, make the following suggestions? First, taking sensible precautions must involve wearing sensible footwear (*not trainers*), gloves and a crash hat. Coats and jackets should be zipped or buttoned up. The horse should be wearing a well-fitting, correctly adjusted lungeing cavesson and, if side reins are being used, these should be attached to a roller and not to the saddle! (However well-balanced the horse, there is always a degree of centrifugal force involved in lungeing and a saddle will inevitably move.)

The equipment should include a purpose-made lungeing whip: I have seen horses chased around with the loop-end of the lunge rein, jumping whips and other totally inadequate 'tools', which are a recipe for lack of control and the pos-sibility of the lunger being kicked. A proper lunge line of adequate length should be used, and any spare line should be evenly coiled and never allowed to drag along the ground. Not long ago, I witnessed a very unfortunate incident in which an owner was dragged when the horse she was lungeing was chased by a loose dog snapping at his heels. She had left the end of lunge line dangling and, when the horse took off, she caught her foot in a particularly long loop. Fortunately, this occurred in a well-fenced manège and the lady's injuries, which could have been much worse, were restricted to severe bruising and a nasty fright. And this brings me to my final point, which is that lungeing should always be carried out on a sound, level surface, in a properly confined area.

So that is the end of my sermon of safety and I hope that all readers will take good care of themselves, their horses – and their saddles.

Appendix 1

THIS SECTION CONTAINS a variety of photos arranged in three broad categories: Aspects of Conformation, Features of Saddlery and Features of Fitting. I have added these for two reasons. First, to provide further examples of the points dealt with in the main text, and to show a few additional features that may be of interest. Second, to encourage readers to observe, identify and form their own views upon various aspects of conformation, saddlery and its fitting. With the latter aim in mind, the captions for these photos are given separately on pages 126–7, to be accessed after readers have formed their own opinions about what is shown. I hope that this layout will help readers to develop an eye for the crucial process of fitting saddles.

Aspects of Conformation

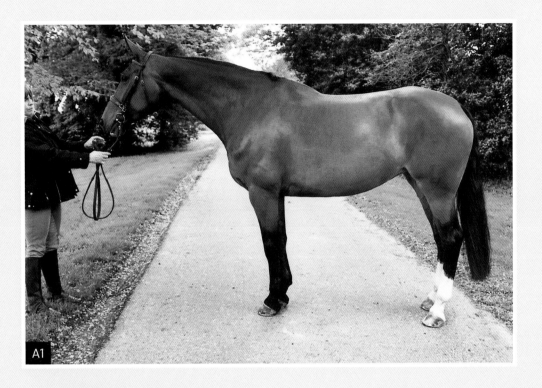

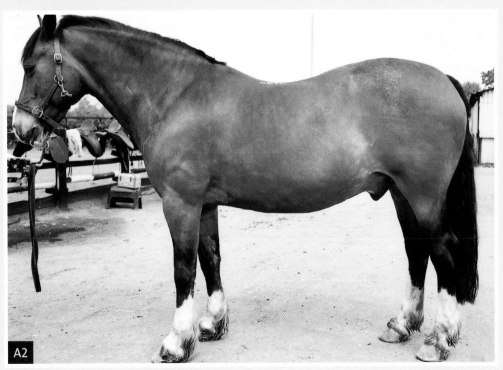

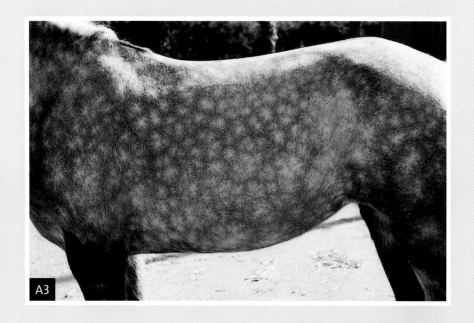

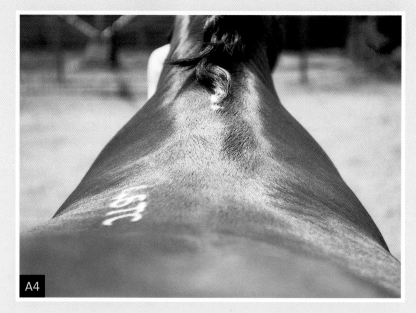

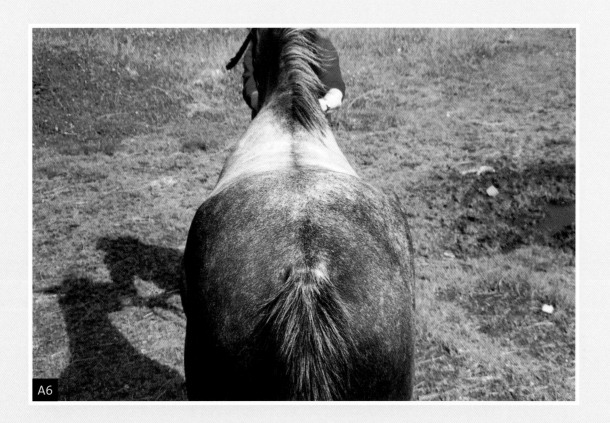

A6

Features of Saddlery

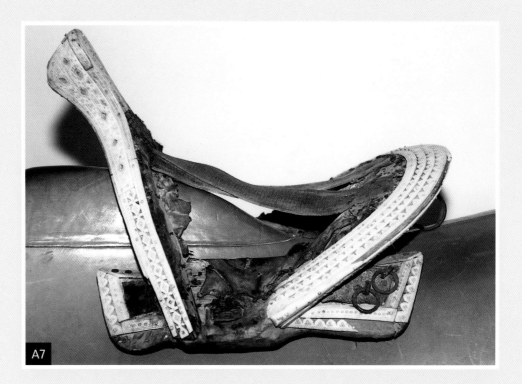

A7

A8

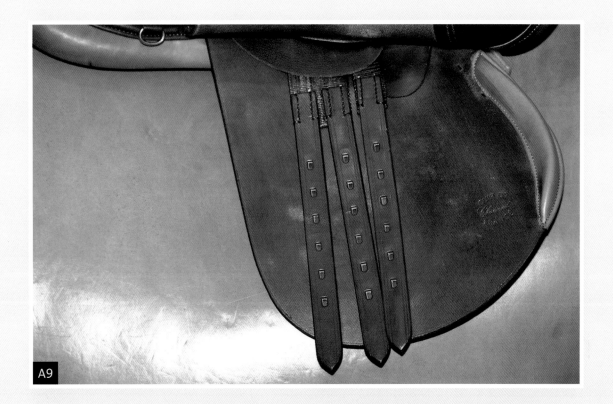

A9

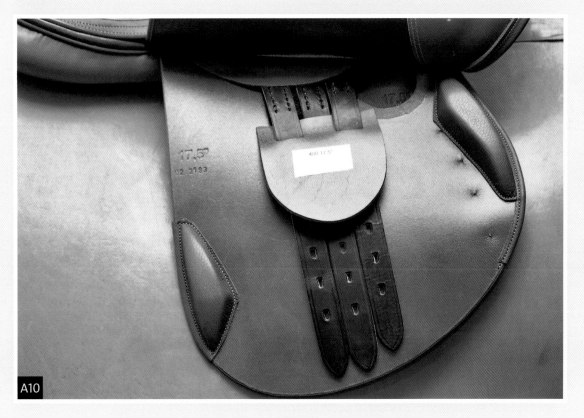

A10

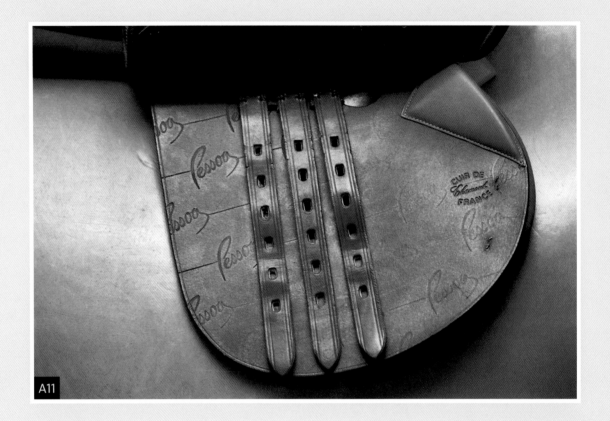

A11

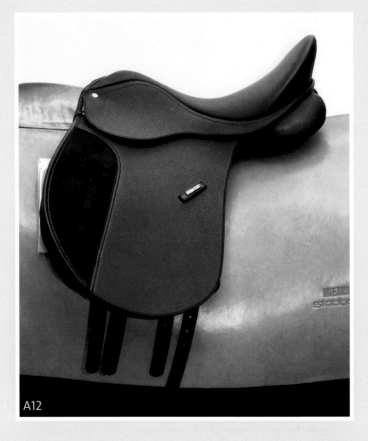

A12

A13

A14

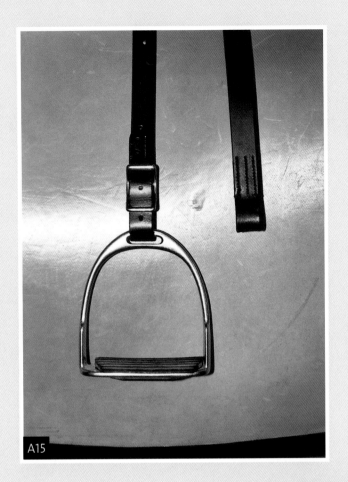

A15

A16

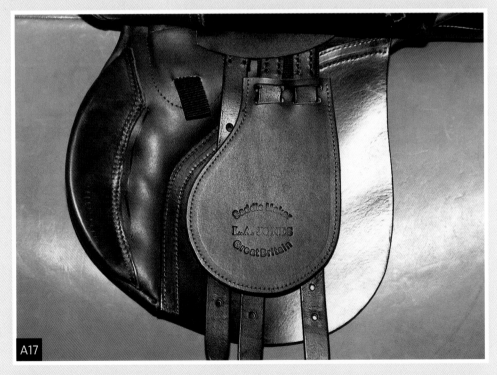

A17

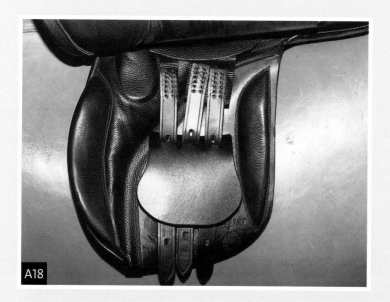

A18

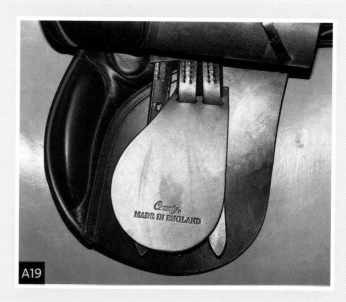

A19

A20

Features of Fitting

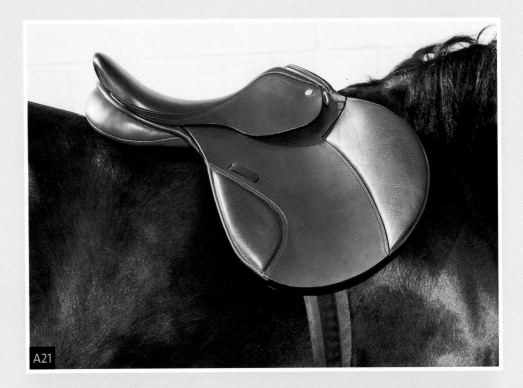

A21

A22

A23

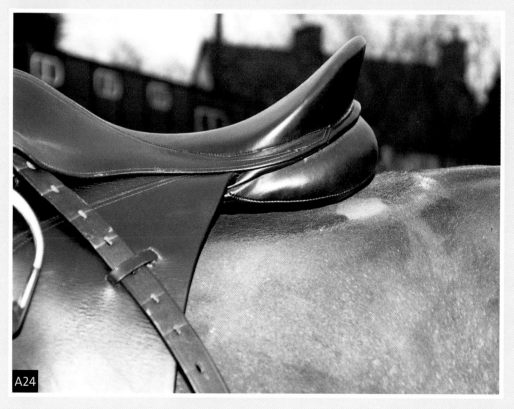

A24

A25

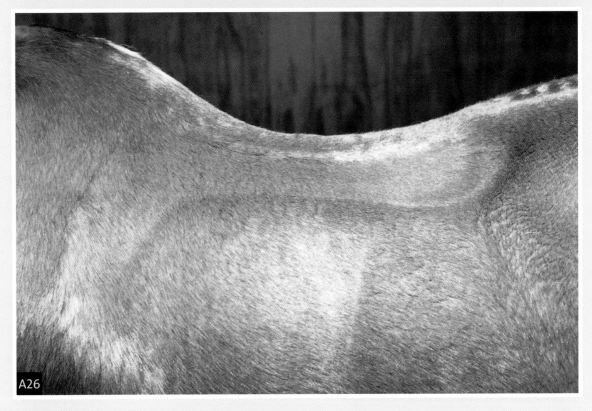

A26

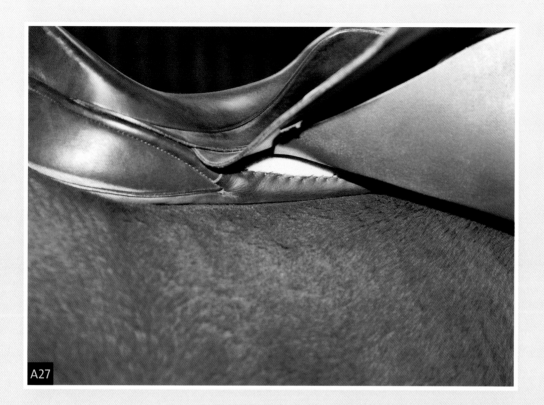

A27

Aspects of Conformation

A1 A nice type of Warmblood, with a good front.

A2 Typical Cob conformation.

A3 A flat back like this would not be suited by a deep-seated saddle.

A4 Another view of a flat back.

A5 Asymmetry can be induced or aggravated by the rider.

A6 A Welsh pony showing marked asymmetry, with much more development on the nearside.

Features of Saddlery

A7 Something out of the ordinary – an antique, ivory-trimmed saddle tree from Arabia.

A8 A saddle with much too narrow a gullet.

A9 Knee roll on a close-contact saddle.

A10 Close-contact sweat flap with upper leg block and thigh roll.

A11 Close-contact sweat flap with upper knee block.

A12 A synthetic general purpose saddle with point and balance billets.

A13 This synthetic saddle is designed with Cobs and native breeds in mind: front point straps and rear balance straps can help prevent forward movement and rear swing and bounce.

A14 An extra-long girth strap designed to prevent girth buckles bulking up beneath the rider's leg.

A15 and **A16**: The stirrup leather system shown in these two photos is often used by dressage riders. It reduces the bulk under the leg by using only one strip of leather rather than two. It has one loop to slide over the stirrup bar and, at the other end, a single loop threads through the stirrup iron onto a buckle adjuster that sits lower than the saddle flap.

A17, A18, A19: Various patterns of buckle guards.

A20 Traditional arrangement of girth straps on a straight-cut saddle with knee rolls.

Features of Fitting

A21 This semi-close-contact saddle sits well in balance but plainly the panel and flap are way too far forward over the shoulder. Not only does this look odd, it must to some degree inhibit the freedom of movement. It is often difficult to fit very forward-cut saddles on Cobs and native breeds.

A22 A semi-close-contact saddle sitting out of balance – too low behind.

A23 Saddle too low behind – rider sitting on buttocks with lower leg too far forwards.

A24 A common problem. Bald patches under rear panel and gussets are often caused by excessive swing and movement in addition to saddles being out of balance, with too much pressure at rear.

A25 Rear of saddle too far back beyond last rib.

A26 Panel marking showing the loaded fit of a new saddle without numnah.

A27 A really nice panel fit.

Appendix 2

This appendix contains a number of questions I devised for quizzes run in conjunction with lectures for Pony Club and Riding Club members and HND students. Readers are invited to use these questions to test their own knowledge.

Answers are on page 130.

Pony Club/Riding Club Quiz

These are all 'Yes' or 'No' answers

1. Should you ever rest your saddle on top of the stable door?

2. Is it the 'grain' side of the saddle that is sealed during the dressing process?

3. Is it possible to over-feed a saddle?

4. Do the horse's shoulder blades move when the horse is in motion?

5. Is it difficult for a saddle fitter to fit a saddle for a big horse and a small rider?

6. Is it difficult for a saddle fitter to fit a saddle for a small horse and a big rider?

7. Is it correct that the horse's loins lie between the last rib and the quarters?

8. If your saddle doesn't fit, can you help rectify the problem by using a numnah?

9. Is it correct to say that all trees are made of wood?

10. Does the colour of your saddle depend on what type of leather was used in its manufacture?

11. Is it true that spring tree saddles can contain as many as several hundred small springs?

12. Are flat-withered ponies easier to fit than ponies with more definite withers?

13. Do close-contact saddles have much deeper seats than other types of saddle?

14. Lots of stirrup irons were once made of nickel, and modern materials aren't nearly so good. Do you agree?

15. Do you agree that wet saddles should be dried off close to a radiator or other form of heat?

16. Is the trapezius the muscle a rider develops in the leg?

17. Is it true that a correctly fitting saddle only comes into contact with the horse's back in two places ñ front and back?

18. Is it true that ageing horses need particular attention paid the fit of their saddles?

19. Is it true that a saddle fitter is more concerned with fitting the horse than the rider?

20. Is it the case that stirrup leathers should stretch with use?

Students' Quiz

1. The majority of UK-made saddles are manufactured in which town?

2. The length of the saddle should not extend beyond the horse's _____?

3. The front of the saddle is called the _____?

4. The back of the saddle is called the _____?

5. What is the minimum number of years it takes to become a Society of Master Saddlers' Qualified Saddle Fitter?

6. Which is the only country to have a non-commercially linked qualification for saddle fitting?

7. What is the minimum number of years it takes to qualify as a Saddler, recognized by the Society of Master Saddlers?

8. Name two types of leather used in saddle manufacture.

9. Saddles are measured in lengths and _____?

10. The width of a saddle is measured where?

11. Well-fitting saddles have large _____ surfaces?

12. Saddles have been in existence for at least how many years?

13. What is the minimum number of years it takes to qualify as a Master Saddler, as recognized by the Society of Master Saddlers?

14. There must be complete clearance of the horse's _____ throughout the entire length of the saddle.

15. When new saddles are being fitted, will the saddle fitter want to see the horse ridden in all or some of the saddles he has short-listed?

And Finally!

Here are some answers given to Trivial Pursuits-type questions that I was asked to devise. In fairness, I should explain that very few of the participants had any involvement with horses. I rather hope that none of them were saddle fitters.

A Girth Is?
– A belt that is used to improve the shape of horses who are too fat, in the same way that corsets improved the figures of Victorian ladies.
– The width of a racecourse.

A Numnah Is?
– Given to horses to numb them when the vet wants to stitch them up.
– The term applied to the way the Egyptians mummified the bodies of their horses.

Stirrups Are?
– What posh people have to drink when they go hunting.

What Helps To Keep A Saddle In Place?
– Straps made of Velcro.
– I think zips are still used sometimes.

A Saddle Skirt Is?
– Used by ladies to preserve their modesty when riding side-saddle.

What is a Pommel?
– It is what is done to a saddle to get rid of the lumps and make it more comfortable for the rider.

Cantle Refers To?
– Going less fast than a gallop.

What Are Withers?
– Marks on an old horse.
– Female horses no longer capable of reproducing.

Pony Club/Riding Club Quiz Answers

1. No, 2. Yes, 3. Yes, 4. Yes, 5. No, 6. Yes, 7. Yes, 8. No, 9. No, 10. No, 11. No, 12. No, 13. No, 14. No, 15. No, 16. No, 17. No, 18. Yes, 19. Yes, ultimately – although the ideal is to fit both, 20. No.

Students' Quiz Answers

1. Walsall, 2. Last rib, 3. Pommel, 4. Cantle, 5. Three, 6. UK, 7. Four, 8. Leathers include pigskin, cowhide, ox hide, calfskin and doe hide, 9. Widths, 10. Gullet, 11. Bearing, 12. 3,000, 13. Seven, 14. Spine, 15. All.

Index

Note: Page numbers in **bold** refer to illustrations